Endorsements for *Winks*

CW00506034

"Told clearly from the heart and with a sense of adventure, *Winks from Above* shares the magic of living with conscious connection to guidance. The book provides practical tips for cultivating and deepening a relationship to highest sources of guidance and conveys hope to draw upon in times of personal trial."

— Joe Gallenberger, PhD, Author of *Inner Vegas, Liquid Luck* and *Heaven is for Healing*

"An entrancing memoir of intuition, natural and learned. We join Liliane for adventures across the continents as well as the inner worlds as she describes the development of her intuitive perception—and how she can help you realize yours. Her life is a demonstration of the power of guardian angels and the knowledge that we, all of us, are not alone."

— Kevin B. Turner, Author, *Sky Shamans of Mongolia: Meetings with Remarkable Healers (Chamanes célestes: Rencontres avec les grands guérisseurs de Mongolie)*

"Filled with amazing adventures, as well as instructive examples of inner guidance at work in her life, Liliane captures your attention and doesn't let go. The range of signs and synchronicities discussed here is sure to raise one's awareness of guidance active in everyday life. Useful tips for inviting even more contact are also included."

— Franceen King, PhD, LMHC, Senior Trainer of *The Monroe Institute*

"This is a special book that reminds us that we are always receiving guidance whether or not we're aware of it. Liliane walks her talk. From a difficult upbringing and life experiences, which has the potential to disconnect anyone from their true nature, Liliane learned to recognize and resonate with her deeper, inner being and expanded sources of guidance. . . leading to incredible healing and transformation. Her story is an inspirational one with many signposts on how the reader can also develop such insights and intuitions and learn to distinguish the difference between anxiety and guidance. Liliane also highlights the importance of resonance with love as the antidote to fear. May it serve you well on your path."

— Luigi Sciambarella, Residential and Outreach Facilitator of *The Monroe Institute* (UK)

"Anyone interested in having a richer, more meaningful, fun, and yes—even a magical—life will want to read Liliane Fortna's *Winks from Above.* It's not often that we come across someone who has been a European model, professional dancer, Amazon explorer, wife, mother, grandmother, energy healer, consciousness explorer, artist, and now, an inspiring author as well, but Liliane embodies all these roles and more.

In her engaging book, Liliane shares events from her extraordinary life, giving many fascinating examples of how she benefitted from getting assistance from what she calls her Guides and Angels during some tremendously difficult and frightful events, as well as how she received helpful guidance on a number of other occasions. By paying attention to the *Winks from Above* —the signs, synchronicities, guidance, and intuitive knowings she experienced—she transformed her harsher life experiences into blessed events, full of positive outcomes.

Liliane gives numerous examples and suggestions of how we can become more conscious of all the signs and messages sent to us by doing such things as reconnecting with our intuition, opening up to communications with our own Guides, and paying attention to the synchronicities which grace us more frequently than we're often aware. If you want to lead a more extraordinary life, read *Winks from Above!"*

> — Nancy H. McMoneagle, Past President and Executive Director of *The Monroe Institute* (Faber, VA)

"Liliane Fortna presents a remarkable book about her international spiritual quest that encompasses an adventurous life of fine art, dance, shamanism, and healing. When she writes about her spiritual endeavors, she has the courage to teach us unabashedly about the Spirits that ongoingly guide her. Through Liliane's accounts, we are reminded that the Spirits are ready to assist us as we learn to work with them. She also teaches us how to address the blocks that self-sabotage our desire to communicate with angels, Spirit animal guides, ancestors, and our dearly departed loved ones on the other side of the veil. Liliane's book is an inspiration, encouraging us to anchor our connection to the messages, to the help, and to the synchronicities offered to us generously by our Spirits."

> — John J. Oliver, Psychic Medium, Star of Court TV's *Haunting Evidence* and Star of *FBI Psychic Investigator* on Nippon Network (Japan)

"Liliane Fortna takes us on an extraordinary journey in *Winks from Above* that beautifully inspires us to know, remember, and embrace that we are all guided by the invisible in our everyday lives. This delightfully written book invites us all to live day to day with this conscious knowing that can open us up to limitless possibilities. She offers many wonderful examples of the magic and support in her life and guides us to begin looking for it in our own. Liliane shows us through her amazing experiences that this is not some special talent only a few have perfected but is the natural state of things and available to all. I highly recommend this to all who are ready to live more full and joyous lives. Thank you, Liliane!"

— Margaretta McIlvaine, *Bridge Between the Worlds Retreat Center,* www.bridgebetweentheworlds.org

Winks from Above

Opening Up to Signs and Synchronicities to Receive Little Miracles Each Day

Liliane Fortna

Published by: Capucia, LLC
211 Pauline Drive #513
York, PA 17402

Paperback ISBN: 978-1-954920-24-8
eBook ISBN: 978-1-954920-25-5
Library of Congress Control Number: 2022905457

Cover Design: Ranilo Cabo
Cover Photo: David Fortna
Interior/Back Cover Author Photos: Jill Meriwether Photography
Layout: Ranilo Cabo
Editor and Proofreader: Lisa Canfield
Book Midwife: Carrie Jareed

Printed in the United States of America

Dedication

To Dave, my Twin Flame

To Kyle and Clara, who are so close to my heart

And to their little Olivia and Amélia, who remind me of the importance of viewing the world with curiosity and wonder

A Note to the Reader

This book contains a wide range of anecdotes that are meant to help you to develop your own ability to identify the many signs from your Spirit Guides (Guides and Angels), interpret those signs and take actions that will result in a richer and happier life.

To encourage you to begin to uncover and expand your capabilities, I provide questions and exercises for you in Parts Two and Three to use as springboards to explore your own history of contact with your Guides and Angels.

I have created a downloadable **Action Guide** as a free companion to this book. It is designed to help you clearly capture and track your personal experiences so that you can better see, interpret, and act on the signs provided by your Spirit Guides. If you wish to receive a copy, you can download and print your **Action Guide** by visiting **www.winksfromabove.com/guide.**

Table of Contents

Author's Notes

Depending on one's education, cultural background, or religious beliefs, many of the terms in this book can be interpreted in a different manner. So, before we begin, allow me to define what these terms mean to me personally and how I interpret them and will use them throughout this book. For more details about the words and terms used, check the Glossary at the end.

Winks from Above

Signs and *Messages* from our *Guides and Angels.*

Synchronicity

An unexpected event when two or more incidents of meaningful coincidences happen at the same time, leading to a positive result. While many view these events as simply "luck" or "chance," to me, they are evidence that I'm not alone, I'm on the right path, and that my *Guides and Angels* are helping me on my life journey, either by providing guidance or by protecting me.

Spirit Guides

The unseen beings who help us, not only in our everyday life, but also when we need it the most. For this book, I refer to them as *Guides and Angels.*

- My **Guides** consist of my main Guide who is constantly with me, and a team of Guides who appear depending on the situation, some of whom might be Ancestors, who provide me with invaluable guidance and wisdom.

1

- The **Angels** consist of my Guardian Angel who protects me, and three Archangels: Saint Michael, Saint Raphael, and Saint Gabriel, who protect and support me during exceptional times.

Your own, personal Spirit Guides will likely be different entities, depending on your upbringing and personal beliefs.

The Veil

The thin partition that separates a person from their Spirit Guides. The thicker and more opaque that partition is, the more difficult the communication. My own veil, at least from my perspective, is almost transparent and sometimes non-existent, keeping my Spirit Guides close by most of the time.

Out-of-Body Experience (OBE)

A very brief period during which a person experiences a sensation of floating outside their body and can usually look at themselves from above or from a short distance away.

Near-Death Experience (NDE)

A life-changing experience during which a person is either clinically dead, near death, or death is imminent. It's not unusual for an OBE to happen during an NDE.

Introduction

This book is about the daily little miracles I call "Winks from Above." These are Signs and Messages placed on our path by our Spirit Guides to communicate with us.

As children, we are very connected with the spiritual, invisible realm, at least until we are taught "grown-up" ways of seeing and interpreting the world around us. When we mature, all those natural links gradually diminish until they are pushed into the deepest recesses of our subconscious mind. There, they remain dormant.

Happily, there are ways to recover these connections and regain our ability to sense and understand what our Guides and Angels are trying to share with us. It's only when we're fully awakened that we're empowered by our innate ability to understand the Winks from Above. Through this, our lives become richer, fuller, and more meaningful.

All of us have had experiences of events, people, animals, objects placed on our path, in ways that seemed out of the ordinary. How did you respond at such times? Did they trigger a reaction causing you to make some changes in your life? Or did you disregard them as too weird, too irrelevant, too demanding?

For most of my life, I have intuitively been able to communicate with the invisible world. I have been blessed to experience many synchronicities and receive answers to questions I have and to desires I want to fulfill. This ability came to me naturally during childhood and has remained that way for most of my adult life. When opportunities arise, I simply follow my inner voice, or my intuition, and go with the flow.

It might be an idea popping into my mind at the exact time I need to find a solution; a sound, a scent or a color that takes me where I need to be; an unexpected but beneficial encounter; an event helping me to be at the right place at the right time; a dream showing me what I have to do or a persistent feeling of what I should or shouldn't do. Imagination is a big part of the process, but it goes beyond that.

Unfortunately, there have also been periods during my adulthood when my intuition was clouded, even blinded by fear, anger, or depression. When our spiritual side is disconnected from our physical side, the natural dialog is interrupted, and we cannot perceive the guidance from Above. During those difficult periods, I know I received Messages from my Guides and Angels because I recorded them in my diary, but I was unable to interpret them or follow their valuable guidance. My intuition was tuned out.

That's precisely where I was when I had to face a frightening medical situation that posed a threat to my health and well-being. After receiving a very unsettling prognosis from multiple specialists, I started searching for answers in all directions. For months, I was plagued by questions about my potential quality of life or even the possible remaining length of my life. I couldn't find anyone to help and felt extremely depressed (although I was determined to hide it from my family). Then, one rainy day, it hit me. Instead of finding out why things were going so wrong, I should be asking myself, *What is the Universe trying to tell me? What is this illness trying to teach me?*

As soon as I changed my focus, I recovered my physical, mental, and spiritual balance, and I was able to renew contact with the Above and regain my understanding of the importance of living in the moment with mindfulness and awareness. Suddenly, Signs and Guidance appeared again and led me to the perfect doctor and medical facility. I even learned the name of my personal Guide, who I can reach out to anytime. He and others have explained in detail many of the events that have shaped my life…and they also led me to write this book!

My month-long, post-operation recovery in the hospital gave me plenty of time to start the process. I was able to acknowledge my good fortune and realize I had been constantly guided throughout the highs and lows of my exciting life. Many "strange" real-life events came to mind, stretching from when I was very young until the present. I wanted to share these stories as examples of how Synchronicity works, with the hope that it might help others realize that they, too, have probably had similar experiences.

This book is for those who have not yet tapped into the wealth of possibilities and rewards offered when you follow the Signs and listen to your Guides. My goal is simple—to help you rediscover those abilities for yourself: reconnect with your intuition and higher self, sense the presence of your Guides and Angels, see and interpret the Signs placed on your path, and take the appropriate actions.

In the following pages, I present a range of actual occurrences, hopefully, to trigger memories of similar (or even totally unrelated) events that may have happened to you.

Let these Winks from Above empower you to lead a better life.

Part 1

While I decided to write this book during my post-operation recovery, initially, I wasn't sure how to begin. However, I soon became convinced that I should use my own story as a starting point.

I realized that, although my childhood and teenage years were very challenging, I survived as well as I did due to my strong, continuous connection with the other side of the Veil, first through my links to Nature as a child and then to art, music, and literature as a teenager. Years later, as an adult, I lost that connection and fell into a severe depression. The treatment that rescued me, based in part on meditation and art and music therapy, helped me find again my ability to use my intuitive senses and to reconnect with my Spirit Guides.

I hope that through sharing my experiences, I can show you the value of being open and paying attention to the Signs and Messages in our lives. By doing so, I hope to motivate you to explore your own life, with an eye toward using these Signs to discover or expand on your own abilities.

So, let's begin with my motivation to do all this—my illness.

CHAPTER 1

Illness

In the summer of 2017, I discovered a lump on the roof of my mouth. It grew very slowly, but steadily, for the following 18 months, and nobody could figure out what it was.

My dentist sent me to an orthodontist, who sent me to an ear, nose, and throat (ENT) specialist, who sent me to a specialist at the ENT department at the local hospital. There, a CAT scan showed a large growth inside the left sinus cavity and a deformation of the left maxillary bone. The lump in my mouth was an extension of that growth. No one could explain what it was, nor if it was cancerous, and I was told the only way to find out was for the doctors to make a hole in the upper palate, explore, then seal it with a removable plug.

I was absolutely incensed that in this day and age, this was the best solution doctors could offer. I asked many times if a probe via the nose or a micro-surgery were possible, but the answer from the doctors was always no, they had to make a hole in my palate to explore and see what it was. However, as it didn't seem to be a malignant growth, they also told me that as long as it didn't bother me, nothing needed to be done—not even a yearly MRI or CAT scan.

A few months later, the lump on the roof of my mouth had grown and was becoming very hard. It had started to cause discomfort when I was eating, so I decided to see another specialist. Frustratingly, he simply pulled my files from the computer, read what had been done a few months before and, without any further analysis, gave me the same verdict as the specialist at the hospital. He even added that in some cases like mine, the teeth and the upper maxillary bone had to be removed, which meant disfigurement with major plastic surgery to follow. Nice!

I was scared and getting very depressed. How come no one could give me an idea of what was wrong with me? Even our family doctor couldn't understand why I was told to do nothing, not even get a yearly scan, unless the lump bothered me. My future seemed bleak no matter which way it went—either my life would end sooner than anticipated or my quality of life would suffer.

But then, not long after that last visit with the specialist, I finally got mad. I became so angry that it made me shift into a combative mode. No more passive me—I was back!

The Search

Over a year and a half had passed since I first saw a doctor regarding the lump in my mouth. I finally realized that since it was obvious no nearby medical facilities could help me, it was time to expand my search outside the area where I lived. I remembered that I had received excellent medical support from several doctors back in Brussels, Belgium, where I had lived for 15 years before moving to Virginia. I decided to contact our family doctor there, hoping he might possibly help me find the right specialist for my condition.

As I made this decision, something shifted in me. I realized for the first time that even as I worked to get more information and a better sense of the future, I should also accept, even prepare for, the worst-case scenario.

However, I never shared this with anybody, even my husband. At the time, I felt that preserving my boundaries was extremely important. Had I shared my feelings with anyone, I feared their attitude toward me might have changed and my resolve to remain strong to the end might have weakened. I just wanted to be treated normally.

Strangely, accepting the potential outcome of my illness made me feel more relaxed and focused. What were my priorities before I became totally debilitated or even had to cross over? How much time would I have? Six months? One year? Two years? To face the ordeal full front and do my very best until the end—this became my goal.

A couple of weeks passed. I was still waiting for an answer from my general practitioner in Brussels and started to wonder if he had retired or changed his email address. That's when something interesting happened. One morning, I drove to our gym under a very heavy downpour. To find a parking spot close to the door was very difficult, but I saw a car ready to leave. I positioned myself to take the spot.

As I sat waiting, a car zipped past me and parked in an empty spot I hadn't noticed, just two cars over. I couldn't believe I hadn't seen it.

That's when, out of nowhere, I realized that I got it all wrong. I had been looking in the wrong direction.

It suddenly became clear that, to solve my medical mystery, I needed to open my eyes, my mind—and extend my search. I had to contact someone other than my former GP. Immediately, the name of the orthopedic surgeon at the Bordet Institute in Brussels, Belgium, came to mind. Six years earlier, Dr. Shumelinsky had successfully removed a very large tumor from my thigh. I emailed him right away to ask for his advice and included pictures from my CAT scans and details about my condition. Only three days later, I received a response. He had already forwarded my email to an ENT specialist who worked in the same hospital. He gave me the number to call to make an appointment.

This was the start of a whole series of Synchronicities, Signs and Guidance from Above.

The Return of Signs and Guidance

As this dreaded-yet-exciting journey finally began, Synchronicities and all kinds of Signs started to appear again.

It began on the way to the airport to fly to Brussels. My husband and I stopped at a local café for a quick bite. We sat on a couch to eat, and on the coffee table in front of us were a few books and magazines. One magazine was left open and out of curiosity I leaned forward to see what the article was about. The title was: "Kick it over!"

I read it as a Message: "Kick your illness over."

Shortly afterwards, in the departure hall of our small airport, I was very surprised to see a huge picture that made me think immediately of St. Michael, who is one of my Guardians. It wasn't an advertisement, just a picture of the Archangel, which was a pleasant but unexpected view at an airport in Virginia! What made it even more bizarre was the fact that just before leaving the house, while I was putting keys I didn't need in a drawer, I came across a keyring with Saint Michael on it. I bought it during one of my visits to Mont Saint Michel in France, but never used it.

I didn't know why, but I decided to take it along and attached it to my carry-on bag.

April 2019 – The First Doctor Visit

There I was in Brussels, at the Institute Jules Bordet, which is renowned for its work with cancer and rare tumors, in front of Dr. Lipski, the ENT surgeon recommended by Dr. Shumelinsky. I had so much hope that he could finally put a name on what I had. He asked a few questions and told me to sit in a chair near one of several machines he had in his office. Before I knew it, an endoscope was going up my nose and down into my sinus cavity. My husband watched the process on a large computer screen.

After the exploration was done, the doctor said, "You have a tumor. Based on its location and growth, it must be removed as soon as possible, and my preference is to do a microsurgery through the nose. It's less traumatic than via the mouth. When I have the results of your MRI and your CAT scan, I'll present your case to our multidisciplinary committee to determine the way ahead. " He added, " To confirm whether the tumor is benign or not, I'll have to do a biopsy. If it is malignant, I might have to go through the roof of the mouth, but I definitely would only remove part of the bone." However, he told me this initial evaluation led him to think that it wasn't malignant, and his preference was to operate through the nose.

Next, he called the nurse who would assist me throughout the process and listed all the appointments she needed to set up for me. It was very comforting to have a surgical nurse assigned to me, to be my point of contact with the surgeon from that day until after the surgery. The nurse swiftly took me to another office where in just a few minutes, I was scheduled for an MRI and a CAT scan for the following week and a biopsy for July, although, depending on the scan results, I was told I might need the biopsy sooner than July. In that case, I'd come back whenever required.

An interesting thing happened while the nurse was lining up my appointments. As I was in the process of putting my phone away, she noticed the logo pasted on the cover of my phone. It is somewhat unique—the symbol of Brittany, the area in France where I grew up. Only someone from that area would recognize it. She asked if I was from Brittany, to which I said "Yes, I grew up there." Well, the nurse turned out to be from the same region. What were the odds? It brought us a bit closer together and made me smile.

Yippee! I was so thankful to have followed the Signs my Guides sent me. It was a Wink from Above.

After months of uncertainty, in only one hour with Dr. Lipski, not only did I get the answer to the question I had been asking for a year and a half, but I also now had greater confidence that the tumor might be benign. And—equally as important—I might not have to lose half of my upper jaw. I left the Institute that day feeling confident that not only I had met the perfect doctor, but I was also at the right medical facility with exactly the right medical staff support.

July 2019 – The Biopsy

The results of my MRI and CAT scans had sadly proven to be inconclusive. My situation appeared to be very complicated. Even though Bordet specializes in difficult and rare tumors, a case like mine had never been seen. *I knew it, I'm an alien!!*

The multidisciplinary medical team that analyzed the scans determined that my tumor could be one of ten or more different kinds of pathology ranging from benign, like a cyst, all the way to cancer. The surgeon told me the next step was to do the biopsy, making a very deep probe via the nasal passage and using microtools to get a good sample of the mass.

During this visit to Brussels, a constant stream of Winks from Above attracted my attention to things I was supposed to see and hear. For instance, after the invasive biopsy, as I was coming around in the recovery room, I was still sedated but feeling surrounded by love and very aware of the people around me. I told the nurse preparing me to be wheeled back to my room that I felt as if I was surrounded by angels. I asked her name, and she answered, "Gabrielle."

Since Saint Gabriel (along with Saint Michael and Saint Raphael) is often present when I need help, I saw this as another Sign.

The news from the pathologists was good. It wasn't cancer. However, although the hospital specializes in the treatment of rare tumors, my ENT surgeon told me that he and the other specialists were quite puzzled; they had never seen anything like this, and he wanted to do more research before deciding on which type of surgery to perform.

The next morning, my orthopedic surgeon Dr. Shumelinsky entered the discussion. He was very familiar with this type of tumor, which is called an *intraosseous hemangioma,* and had removed many, although he had never seen or heard of such a tumor appearing in the jaw area. He told me he would do his best to be present to observe the operation and even help if needed.

Once again, I felt I was in very good hands and knew my Guides were walking beside me.

I left the hospital just in time to celebrate the Belgium National Day, a two-day event full of activities with a beautiful parade attended by the King and the Queen. After the parade, as my husband and I were enjoying mussels (a Brussels specialty) on the terrace of a very busy restaurant, the couple sitting next to us started chatting with us. They both spoke English fluently. She was an artist who also happened to be very well versed in the medical system in Belgium and the U.S., in part because many members of her family were doctors. He was a retired surgeon who worked for the Belgian Ministry of Health and who traveled frequently to the U.S. to give lectures. His specialty: *the jaw! What were the odds?* We chatted late into the night and watched the magnificent fireworks that concluded the festivities. They invited us for dinner at their beautiful home before we returned to the States.

What were the odds of meeting such a lovely couple who could perfectly understand what I was going through and could advise me about the medical system in Belgium?

The Synchronicities continued throughout my stay. Every day offered many beautiful opportunities. I felt so thankful to my Guides for their love, support, and help. It was as though I was gliding or being carried from one event to the next rather than being pulled, pushed, and shoved to move forward.

After the biopsy, I was not allowed to fly for another two or three weeks, which gave me time to rediscover Brussels. I happened to be there at a very special time, because the town was celebrating the 450th anniversary of the artist Bruegel's death. I decided to go to one of the major exhibits to see *The Fall of the Angels*, depicting the Archangel Michael leading the charge against the Devil's army. On the way, I noticed all the ancient, wrought iron streetlights and traffic poles that lined the old center streets, protecting the pedestrian sidewalks. On each of them was an effigy of Saint Michael! Curious now, I looked around and noted that all the city trash cans and lamp poles, also made of wrought iron, included the Archangel's image. Having been away from the city for several years, I had forgotten that Saint Michael is Brussels' patron saint. Remember, as I already mentioned, this Archangel is one of my main Guardians. Standing there in the street, I was hit with the realization that I was literally surrounded by his support and presence. This sense of protection carried me through the rest of my recovery in Belgium and my subsequent return a couple of weeks later to my Virginia home.

After spending about two months at home, it was time to return to Brussels. We arrived a few days before the surgery. Just after checking into the hotel, another Wink from Above made my day. I was going to call the elevator to go down to the lobby. I reached for the button but before I could touch it, the door opened. To my surprise, no one was there. Puzzled at first, I walked in and pressed on the button to go down the four floors. I thought that maybe I should ask someone at the front desk if it was normal that when you just stand in front an elevator, the door opens before you even press to call for it. I had spent a lot of time in that hotel, and it had never happened before. But before I got to the front desk, it dawned on me that it was a Wink from Above. I smiled and decided to keep this little episode to myself and thanked my Guardians for reminding me that I was not facing this challenging time in my life alone.

"Good morning!" I said to the clerk as I placed my key on the counter. "Have a wonderful day!" I walked away still smiling.

October 2019 – The Operation

I checked into the hospital, with the surgery scheduled for the next morning. I knew it was going to be experimental and very invasive. The surgeons would not know how radical the procedure would have to be until they started working on the tumor. If Plan A didn't work, there was still the risk that they would have to remove some or much of my upper jaw and most of my upper teeth. Nonetheless, I was not feeling especially nervous. Rather, I was full of gratitude for the amazing series of events over the previous several months that had led me to that point. I knew everything would go very well. After all, I was going to be operated on by the best surgeons I could have; Dr. Lipski, the ENT surgeon, Dr. Digonnet, the head of the Cervico-facial Surgery Department, and Dr. Shumelinsky, who had already successfully removed a rare tumor I had several years prior.

Their plan for my operation was quite complicated. In an attempt to save my teeth and upper jaw, the surgeons were going to operate simultaneously, one through the mouth and one through the nose. Dr. Lipski would perform a micro-surgery via the nasal/sinus passage to first remove the part of the tumor that was inside the sinus cavity. Then, he would drill a hole in the upper palate to remove the rest of tumor, which was lodged in the bone itself. At the same time, Dr. Digonnet would operate on the upper palate via the mouth.

Both surgeons would begin by cutting and rolling back the membranes from, respectively, the sinus cavity and the roof of the mouth. Since Dr. Shumelinsky specialized in this specific type of tumor, he would monitor their progress. Once the tumor was fully removed, the quarter-sized hole remaining in the upper palate had to be filled. Instead of using a graft, Dr. Lipski would use part of the septum, the cartilage found in the central part of the nose, placing it in the hole and sealing it into place on the sinus cavity side with the mucus membrane. On the mouth side, Dr. Digonnet would do the same with the upper mouth membrane.

I should note that this type of surgery had never been attempted—Dr. Lipski created it specifically for my situation. If it failed, a major part of the upper maxillary bone and many of my upper teeth would have to be removed. This was an extremely unpleasant prospect. It would mean that my face would have to be opened from the corner of the left eye, down the left side of the nose, around the nostril to below the nose and the upper lip. Months of extensive plastic surgery would then be required. But I felt confident that it would not go that far. I had great faith in the doctors.

Early on the morning of the operation, I meditated and got ready for the surgery. I indulged myself to go online to check messages from my loved ones and friends. On my Facebook page was a graphic with the words: "Let it go. It will dissipate."

Was that a Wink from Above?

While I was in the bathroom brushing my teeth, thinking it could possibly be the last time my mouth would be intact, I heard my husband come into my room and opened the door to greet him. Looking out at the panoramic view of the city through the windows behind him, I spotted a very thick, dark plume of smoke billowing from an area not far from the nearby train station. The cloud rapidly got thicker and was pushed to the left by the wind. Then, in about 15 minutes, it was gone. There was not a trace of the heavy smoke. All was clear. That was odd. What did it mean? I smiled as I realized it was probably a Sign that echoed the Message I saw earlier on the Internet. *Let it go. It will dissipate.*

I was also quite amused when I saw three crows pass by the window. One landed on a roof just below while two continued chasing each other. This was a very good omen. The crow is my Animal Spirit.

While being wheeled down to the surgery room, I felt very peaceful and ready to face whatever would come my way. I closed my eyes and right away, I saw Saint Michael on my left, Saint Raphael on my right, Saint Gabriel leading the way. My husband was walking behind my bed.

How did I recognize the Archangels? Honestly, I don't know, but I did. They've been with me for quite a long time, and I can feel their presence, especially when I need them.

After the 5 ½ hour surgery, when I started to regain consciousness, the first thing I did was move my tongue to feel if my upper left teeth were still there. It was thrilling to feel them. That meant the drastic surgery had been avoided. It meant my face hadn't been cut open from the inner corner of my left eye down to below the nose and upper lip. It meant the bone and teeth hadn't been removed. And it meant I wouldn't need reconstructive surgery. I was thrilled and thankful—in a groggy kind of way. Dr. Lipski's head popped in from behind the curtain and while giving him a thumbs up, I told him, probably in a very drowsy voice, "You see, Doctor, it all went very well." I felt so full of gratitude that he had created a surgery that had never been done. Until the last minute, he didn't even know if it would work.

It dawned on me that prior to the surgery I was surrounded by the excellent number Three:

- Three crows - my Animal Spirit, playing in front of my window an hour or so before surgery
- Three Archangels appearing when I was wheeled to the surgery room
- Three surgeons
- Three assistant doctors
- Three anesthesiologists

I also felt so full of gratitude to be surrounded by the loving presence of my husband, the love of my family, friends, the Energy Healing community, and the constant support of all my Guides, my Guardian Angel and even my three Archangels.

The Recovery

For one month, a tube connected to a feeding pouch snaked down into my stomach via my nose. It was certainly not the most pleasant situation. Still, I started each day feeling full of gratitude and joy. This reflected the relationship I had with all the people taking care of me. I felt they were more like friends than caretakers. When time allowed, nurses would linger in my room to chat. The massage therapist would come every afternoon to make me more comfortable. A team comprised of a speech therapist, a nutritionist and a dietician would make sure I was ingesting the right amount of food—first via the pouch, then pureed food to help me gradually transition to solids. The speech therapist made sure I could move the food around my mouth properly and that I could swallow with no problem, and the nutritionist and the dietician would adapt my meals according to what I could or couldn't ingest. There was nothing negative about those sessions. All the ladies had great personalities and made it very interesting and fun.

Two young doctors would drop by once or twice a day to check on me, and if I needed some related medical issue to be checked while in the hospital, someone would wheel me down to the lab or office where I was supposed to go. Volunteers from the Friends of the Hospital would drop by in the afternoon to offer coffee, tea, hot cocoa, and cookies. At first, I had to refuse because I couldn't eat or drink anything except the contents of the feeding pouch, but it was pure joy the day I could start accepting such delightful afternoon treats, always offered with kindness and a smile.

Last but not least was the outpouring of support from friends sending me Healing Energy and Love.

All was in place for me to recuperate and heal fast. I was so grateful to receive so much from this side of the Veil…but also from my Spirit Guides on the other side.

I had only asked for a private room. I don't know how, but I had the "luck" to be assigned to the best room on the top floor. It was at the end of the long single corridor, away from the noise. That end of the building is semi-circular, so the outside wall of the room contained a large bay window with a sprawling, curved view of the city. Because my room was located on the eighth floor of a hospital that stands taller than the surrounding buildings, the view from this panoramic window was beautiful and fascinating. Lying in my bed, it always brought me so much joy to observe the movements of the clouds and the variation of colors throughout the day. It was very conducive to connecting with my Guides. It also was quite entertaining be able to immerse myself in this part of the old Brussels. The most intriguing sight was a beautiful tower nearby. It's the only remaining 13th century gate tower from the wall originally surrounding the city.

The beautiful view from my hospital bed of the 13th Century tower.

One night, the full moon woke me up. It was magnificent. I noticed a couple of windows of the massive, multi-floor tower were lit. I wondered if the building, now a museum, was guarded at night. Another night, I woke up around 3:00 a.m. and lights were on in a couple of windows of the tower, but I noticed they were not in the same area where I had seen them before. I took pictures to show the nurses the next day, thinking they might have an explanation. However, nobody was able to give me a clear answer, except that they didn't believe anyone was in the building after closing time.

Night after night, at least one light was on, sometimes in one of the stairwells, sometimes in one of the rooms on a different floor. It was strange. The lights were always in different sections of different floors, and they would be on and off at different times. Although unusual, I found this nighttime entertainment surprising and amusing. I wondered if a guard was watching over the tower, or if my Spirit Guides were "Winking" at me from the windows. After all, I wasn't sleeping well. It was a bit uncomfortable trying to sleep with a feeding tube inserted into my nose and going all the way down into my stomach!

A couple of days after the surgery, the three-foot-long tube was dislodged during the night. Believe me—it was no small thing to re-insert another one! I was a bit concerned that it would happen again, and that kept waking me up. Those on and off lights moving around the old tower were strange, but I felt they were Winks from Above to remind me that I was not alone, and all was well. I was rather disappointed when I didn't see them at least once during the night.

The day after I was discharged from the hospital, my husband and I went to visit the museum inside the tower. I wanted to find out more about the "nightly entertainment" seen from my bed. The lady sitting behind the ticket counter seemed nice, so I asked her if someone was guarding the tower during the night. When she said no, I explained to her that I had just spent a month in the hospital across the street and from my room, during the night, I could see lights in different areas of the building, and that they were going on and off at different times. She said she never heard of such a thing, but she was starting to mention that some visitors had expressed feeling uncomfortable while visiting the Tower and had to leave very fast. A male colleague who was sitting nearby seemed unhappy she was giving me so much information. He interrupted her abruptly and told her in an unfriendly tone there were people waiting to buy tickets.

To me, this indicated that there was definitely "something" in the tower that no one should talk about. I decided to find someone else to get more information. The next day, I returned to the tower, went straight to the gift store, and asked the woman behind the counter the same question. She too said she never heard of anything like that and suggested I should talk to the manager. As she was saying that, the manager happened to be crossing the store to go to the elevator. *What were the odds?* The saleswoman introduced us, and I told the manager my story. She, too, insisted nobody stayed in the building after closing time and there were no security lights. I told her I could prove that what I saw was real and I had pictures with me to prove it. To which, she said, in a very light tone, "Oh, maybe they're ghosts." With that, she walked as rapidly as she could toward the elevator.

Three months later in February, I was back in Brussels for a post-surgical check-up. Since I had time between the CAT scan appointment and the visit with the surgeon, my husband and I decided to go to Paris for the day—it's only an hour and 20 minutes away by bullet train. We got up very early, long before sunrise, to be at the train station by 6:30. The station was not far from our hotel, so we decided to walk, which took us right by the 13th century tower. As we approached the building, I jokingly wondered aloud if my Spirit Guides would give me a Wink from Above. It was still dark, and as we were approaching, I thought I saw a light in one of the side windows. My husband said it probably was the reflection of the streetlights. I couldn't really tell but assumed he probably was right. However, as we passed in front of the main entrance, we both saw that way up on the top floor, the window was brightly lit. This was strange, since, during my "investigation," I had been told the staff didn't come in early. And even if someone had come in at that ungodly hour, wouldn't there be light in the stairwell, not just the uppermost floor?

I suppose it was a Wink from my friends Above to let me know they were still with me, even months after my surgery. I smiled and continued to walk to the train station.

This challenging episode of my life made me realize that I have to share with others how they too can seek and receive what they need. The ability to recognize Signs from Guides and Angels is not a gift that only a few chosen ones possess. It's an innate ability we all have.

Including you.

Facing a potentially debilitating illness for over a year and a half, I was scared and depressed, contemplating how many months or years I might have in front of me and whether I would end up disfigured. I felt lost and totally abandoned by my Spirit Guides. But everything started to change when I made peace with myself, accepted the ultimate outcome, and finally surrendered. Only when I was ready to face whatever was thrown at me and even started to list all I wanted to accomplish before crossing over did the Signs reappear. Then I was able to reconnect with my Spirit Guides, see and interpret Signs, and ultimately find the answers I was seeking.

CHAPTER 2

Early Childhood

I was born in Hanoi, Vietnam in March of 1949, in the midst of the French-Vietnamese War to a French father and a Vietnamese mother. Vietnam was then part of Indochina, a French colony. A few months later, Mao Tse-Tung came to power, and it became a time of political turmoil. Many feared the Chinese were ready to cross the border (only 90 miles away) to invade Vietnam. Hanoi was also plagued by waves of epidemics that had already claimed the lives of many children. As a safeguard, my parents decided to send me to live with my paternal grandmother in Brittany on the coast of France—for a short while, they thought.

As far back as I can remember as a child, I was always straddling the border between this world and the unseen one. My childhood was difficult. My grandmother had so much hardship to bear when I came into her life at age 15 months that I became her emotional—and sometimes physical—punching bag. She would yell at or hit me for any reason. Very early on, this made me more aware of the importance of observing my world with my whole being. I started to notice signs of what could potentially become dangerous for me. The tone in my grandmother's voice, a word she said, the look on her face, the way

My mother and I (4 months old) in Hanoi, Vietnam.

she breathed, and her body language gave me all kinds of indications whether I was in trouble and needed to be ready to escape.

My grandmother had alienated everyone around her, even her own children. The highlight of my very early childhood was when we would visit my aunts, uncles, and cousins in Nantes, which was about one hour away by bus, or when they came to visit us. To be with them always meant lots of hugs, games, and laughter. But one day, when I was around five, my grandmother informed me that they were thieves, and I would never see them again. It made me very sad, for although I had not seen them too often, Uncle Louis, Aunt Marie-Claire, and my little cousin Gilles were the kindest people I knew. In retrospect, they probably also were the only ones who gave me a sense of what a normal family was like. A year or so later, they came to visit me at my school after classes and told me how much they had missed me. Their visit made me feel so warm and happy. After they parted and I started walking home, I was sure my grandmother would forgive whatever they had done wrong, because the box of chocolates they had given me was so big and so beautiful...I never had received such a gift. Well! It was a silly thought. I was ordered at once to throw the box and its contents in the garbage. "I'm sure they have poisoned them," she said. The next time I saw any of my aunts, uncles, or cousins was twenty-one years later, in 1976.

I never saw a doctor, a dentist or got medication from a pharmacy until age nine, when I started boarding school near Paris. My grandmother would prepare concoctions she made with plants. "Mind over matter" was always what I was encouraged to do. It's called the "Coué method." I learned to use positive thoughts as a healing power. I remember when I had the whooping cough. It was very painful and when I coughed during the night, my grandmother would scream at me to be quiet and hit me as soon as I started to cough again.

I was prevented from playing with other children, so I wasn't aware of what the norm was. Of course, I was in contact with children during

When I was about 3 years old, near where I grew up in Brittany.

school, but sometimes my grandmother asked the nuns to keep me in the dining hall during recess, just because she had decided I shouldn't play with others. And since we didn't go to church on Sundays, I was quite isolated. However, children are very resilient. When they can't compare their life with the lives of others, they cope. They don't miss what they don't know. There was no TV or means to see how others lived. It's only when I was able to read that I started to discover ways of life very different from mine.

I was very fortunate to be surrounded by Nature. It became my refuge and helped me soothe my pain when life became difficult. I lived next to the beach, and across the road was a path leading to the woods, fields, a creek, and a little pond. When in Nature, I communicated with the trees, the flowers, the animals, and the insects.

The outline shows the beautiful place where I lived until age nine. The house on the left was our home. It's been renovated throughout the years and is now twice as big as when I lived there. The walls and crenellated towers surrounding the garden and the manor are still like they were then. The whole area seems to be frozen in time.

Food was not only scarce, it also was, for me, a source of punishment. Sometimes, when it was very hot outside, and I was thirsty, my grandmother prevented me from drinking anything. But there was a faucet in the garden, and I learned to find my own food on the rocks beyond the small beach. In season, oysters became a staple, and mussels and barnacles too. I usually carried a little knife but observed that if I was fast enough, when it was going to rain, I wouldn't need it. I could detach the barnacles from the rock with my fingers. The variety of pines growing in the area were also a great source of nutrition, providing me with delicious pine nuts. I never got sick from what I ate. At that time, there was no pollution on the seashore.

I remember during the warm months, when I came across hydrangea bushes, I loved to put my face into the large flowers, slowly moving against the cool petals and imagining tiny fingers caressing my eyes, cheeks, nose, and forehead. It felt so wonderful and soothing.

The full moon and starry sky would always take me to another world, a beautiful world where all was possible. It would take me to where I would feel warm inside—as if I were wrapped in a cocoon infused with love. Not that I had ever experienced love directed toward me, but I had observed the ways people looked at each other with kindness.

For a while, there was a spider on the ceiling just above my bed. When I silently talked to her, she lowered herself by about a foot and stayed there until our conversation was over. Then she went back up. I don't know how long this lasted, but it was fun for me to have that special little friend. Apart from vipers, I hadn't learned yet to be afraid of any insect or animal. They never hurt me. I was actually much more cautious around people.

At night, the owls would always sing their sorrowful songs. There was a large tree right next to the staircase leading to our front door, and sometimes, on a branch very close to the landing, an owl would hoot and seem to look at me. In my mind, I would join her and follow her on her nightly flights. Lying in bed, I would listen to the sea, and when it wasn't a windy night, the ebb and flow of the tide made me think of a slow, deep breath. It would lull me to sleep. Nature's lullaby helped me drift into a beautiful world.

Crossing the Border

It wasn't until much later in life that I understood I was guided, watched over and supported by my Guides and Angels. However, from the time I arrived as an infant in France, they were helping me via the bounty and the beauty of Nature and the love and fun that animals brought into my life. Like all children, I never questioned who they were. It felt natural to "talk" and listen to the Spirits of Nature and anything animate or inanimate that was part of my surroundings. I never felt alone when I spent time by myself on the beach, in the woods or in the garden.

It was very easy for me to connect with the other side. It was such a natural state, I never considered that it might not exist. My grandmother was an ultra-religious Catholic. I went to catechism, but not to church, because my grandmother didn't want to talk to most of the other villagers. However, even though she only went to church once or twice a year, the Virgin Mary, Jesus, and the Saints were always omnipresent. "Do not whistle, it will make the Virgin Mary cry." "Pray to Saint Antony, he will help you find what you lost." She covered religious pictures or statues when I had to undress. I was always told that on Good Friday, the church bells stop ringing because they go to Rome, and when they return on Easter Sunday, they fly above houses and gardens and drop chocolates for the good children. I knew I wasn't one of them because I never found anything in the garden, but I swear, I truly believed I saw the bells pass above us at least once.

There was a constant blur for me between reality and non-reality. The two intermingled on a linear plane and I never thought to make a distinction. Although I felt guided throughout my childhood, I took for granted all the experiences and ease with which I would connect. I never talked to others, especially my grandmother, about my feelings and experiences. The way I felt wouldn't have settled very well with her and might have gotten me into trouble. After all, the friendly entities I connected with were not part of the Catholic church. So, I kept everything to myself. Inanimate objects such as rocks, clouds, the wind, the sea and animate ones such as insects, birds, dogs, cats, trees, and flowers were part of my world. I interacted with them constantly. They were, in many ways, my imaginary friends and my teachers.

Every year, during the summer months, it was such a joy to observe the long procession of ants going from their nest at the bottom of a big tree and making a long trail further into the garden. I would lie down for hours, it seemed, and watch them interact with one another. Sometimes, it was amazing to see two or three help each other with a burden too heavy and bulky for just one of them to carry. I noticed the type of grains they took back home, and I sometimes would trick them by placing a different type of grain on their path. I would talk to them, and they oftentimes would stop and investigate my offering. Sometimes they dropped their load and two or three of them would cooperate to carry the new item. They were, to me, like tiny people going back and forth doing hard work. I observed how determined they were to take home what they were carrying, and how they would cooperate and work together.

TV wasn't part of my world, but I didn't miss anything. Nature around me was a constant source of fun discoveries. As I didn't have much opportunity to be with people, I learned a lot from observing even the tiniest creatures living in the garden.

Raised without Love

I have always experienced extreme sensitivity whenever anything comes in contact with my throat—something I used to assume was related to a past life. I had been told that I probably was a witch during the Middle Ages and before being burned at the stake, I had been strangled.

I researched and found out that indeed such a practice existed. If the witch had money, she could pay her executioner to strangle her before the fire started.

However, more recently, I learned that the discomfort I feel around my throat comes from the time my grandmother nearly strangled me. Before a meal, she would tie my napkin around my neck, as was the norm for children and adults in France. However, on this occasion, she was very angry at me and pulled on both ends of the cloth so forcefully that I couldn't breathe. I must have been very young to not be able to tie the napkin myself. I can still remember putting my hands to my throat to try to loosen the napkin, gasping for air, and the sound it made. Then, nothing, just the vision of standing about six feet away to the left of the little girl, watching her struggle as she couldn't breathe. I don't recall how it ended, but I'm convinced now that it was a Near-Death Experience (NDE). It's not unusual to have an Out-of-Body Experience (OBE) during an NDE.

The positive aspect of this recent discovery is knowing that the sensitivity I experience on my throat is from the muscle memory of being strangled. That is something I can work on energetically and totally rid myself of. Why didn't I find out about it earlier in my life? Honestly? Until recently, I never thought of asking my Guides about the sensitivity of my throat.

As a child, I would often compare my grandmother's size to mine and stand next to her to see how much I had to grow to be as tall as or taller than she. The few times people saw that, they commented on how sweet it was. I would just smile. Little did they know that deep inside, I was angry, and it was slowly getting worse. What I really had in mind was that I couldn't wait to be taller and stronger so I could hit her back. It was very unhealthy to think that way and I'm glad I had catechism once a week. It probably kept my moral compass on track, showing me the right direction to go, and keeping me out of trouble.

More than the teachings of the church, what helped me most was the beauty of my surroundings. When things were rough inside the house, I would go outside and sit or walk on the beach or the rocks. The sound of the ocean and the caress of the breeze would soothe me. When in the evening I could sit on the rock at the bottom of the garden, the sunset would fill me with so much beauty deep inside that sometimes I felt like crying out in joy. After nightfall, the star-constelled sky was also such a source of awe. I felt so small, yet at the same time, when I would immerse myself in the immensity of the sky, I felt one with the Universe. I would talk to my imaginary friends up there. I never needed to say much, for I knew they understood.

Still, it wasn't always easy to be all alone. Especially when I had to deal with my grandmother's anger. I had Nature and its abundance, but to have very little interaction with other children and no warm touch from a human being was not always easy. Since contact with others was limited, I didn't have a lot of opportunities to observe how people behaved with one another. I didn't know that hands could help soothe or provide tenderness through caresses and holding. The only hands I was able to observe very closely were my grandmother's hands. They were very wrinkled, hard and would never provide any form of tenderness. Instead, they would often hit me on any body parts they could reach. However, I must have observed some tenderness through what I saw during the few visits with the people my grandmother was in contact with. Some of the villagers were kind to me, but not very close. I always felt a distance between them and me. Of all the houses in our village, there were only a few I was allowed to enter, and we never received anyone.

In France, paid vacations were established in the mid-fifties; that's when in August families started to come to the beach. From my private nook at the top of the two crenelated towers bordering the corners of our garden, I observed how people interacted. That's when I realized so much was alien to me.

The tenderness parents would show their children, the games they played, all the wonderful laughing and joy they exhibited—I would so much have loved to experience it too! I craved hugs and nice words from my grandmother, but they never came.

Although, while I may have missed the human touch, I don't remember ever being bored. I had no toys, but Nature always provided me items to create with. The squid's bones would become little boats when I inserted a wood stick in the middle to make a mast; the fuchsia flowers were little dancers; I would make a bow and arrows with small branches I found on the beach and run around fighting invisible enemies—there was so much to observe and to marvel about.

My Animal Guides

The parish priest had a little dog named Cappi, and for a while, he came every school day to visit me. He would show up and bark to announce himself by our garden door every morning to take me to school. I never understood how he knew when it was time for me to leave, for he was always there on time. And then, in the afternoon, after school, he sat right by the big school gate and stood up, tail wagging, as soon as he saw me. I don't remember how long he did this, but it was long enough that it remains one of my most heartwarming memories from those times when I needed a friend.

I would always walk to school by myself. I didn't mind because I would walk along the beach, or when the wind was too strong, through the wooded area. But I remember that sometimes, as I was approaching the school, children would call me names such as "boite a cirage" (shoe polish box), because of my skin color, or "Chinetoque" (a derogatory name for Chinese or Asian people). Even though I wouldn't let other children tease me or call me names, and I would often fight back, it was still comforting to have my four-footed companion escorting me to school.

What puzzles me even to this day is that this dog wasn't interested in playing. I tried many times to engage him to have fun, but it was as if he had a duty to fulfill—to escort me to school and back to my house. He wasn't distant, he enjoyed it when I petted him, but he just wasn't playful.

I'm sure he was sent by my Guardian Angel to help me through this difficult phase.

Since I was raised by my grandmother who abused me physically, I hadn't experienced much warm, human contact—except for those infrequent visits from my aunt and uncle during my early years. It was rare for me to be allowed to speak or play with other children, so any interaction with Nature and animals was always welcomed. I had a special bond with another neighborhood dog named Moulouk, a tall black dog with pointy ears, who often came to visit me. He was a poor, wretched creature, mistreated by his owner, especially when she was drunk. We spent what seemed to be hours at a time playing on the beach, wading in the water, eating oysters and mussels on the rocks or, when the tide was high, playing in the woods on the other side of the road. And when I was craving tenderness, which I had rarely experienced, Moulouk gave me, in a different form, the warmth I was looking for. To rest on his belly felt like I was cradled by someone who loved me.

One day, since I hadn't seen him for a while, which was unusual, I decided to find out what happened. As I was walking up the path leading to his house, I saw him lying in the dirt. I called out, but he did not respond. I found it very strange that he did not move, for he had been my friend for as many years as I could remember, and he was always very excited to see me. A closer look showed me he was tied up beside the front door of his house and had become very skinny and dirty. As I approached him, he barely moved. He lifted his head a bit, wagged his tail slightly but seemed unable to get up. His hair was matted, and his ribs were showing quite a lot. His owner had beaten him to the point that a bone protruded from a big gash on his side. I didn't know what to do, except pet him and quietly talk to him. There was nobody I could ask for help, and I was very afraid the owner would come out and tell my grandmother I was trespassing.

The next day, I was home and heard a dog howling at the end of the road. I looked and saw my wounded friend standing right in the curve of the road. I ran up to see him, but he had already disappeared into the woods. The following day, a man said he found Moulouk dead, lying near the pond in the woods—a place where he and I went quite often. I don't know how he managed to escape and where he found the strength to walk so far. But I do know my best friend came to say goodbye and then went to the place he and I visited often, a special place where we had fun and peace, away from those who mistreated us.

To this day, I cannot think about Moulouk and his last days without a tug in my heart. He came into my life at a time when I had no friends and rarely had the opportunity to play with other children. His frequent visits were always a great source of joy. Although he was not ours, he must have spent a lot of time with me, for I remember him as almost a constant companion.

I'm convinced he was sent to me by my Spirit Guides not only to help me survive years of my difficult childhood but also to learn love and compassion. I was going to catechism and learning about love and kindness, yet it's not what I could observe around me. I had a hard time trusting people.

Crows were omnipresent in our area, and I recognized their excited *caw caw* when something edible had washed up on the shore. I would run through the garden and down the few steps to the beach to where the birds were gathering. I don't know why, but the bounty would almost always wash ashore in the same area. As I approached, a few of the birds would fly away, and there was always enough for all of us. I would quickly grab a squid or two or whatever had just washed up on the sand, then I would run back home to give them to my grandmother, hoping it would help her and she would be happy with what I brought home to eat.

Decades later, I found out that the crow is my Animal Spirit, and I was not too surprised by the discovery.

One winter, my grandmother was cat-sitting for a lady who spent that part of the year in Provence. It was of course a delight for me to have a constant little friend who brought me so much joy. Pèpète the cat slept with me and was always nearby except when I went to the beach. One day, an accident happened to her while my grandmother was making crêpes. Our wood stove was the very old style, with rings that could be removed or added, depending on the heat needed to cook. Very curious, Pèpète would stand on my grandma's shoulders and watch the crêpe being flipped, flying up and then being caught by the skillet on the way down. She sometimes tried to catch it as it was flying high. It was so cute and funny to see! But one day, she lost her balance and landed with her four paws on the burning stove. We heard a piercing scream as she bolted out of the house into the garden. She was nowhere to be seen and we were afraid she would never come back. Then a few days later, we heard her outside; she was hiding under a bush and still didn't want to come close. So, we brought her food and water. It took quite a while for her to come back home and act like she did before.

I sat near the bush and talked to her. I understood so well that she was in pain and wanted to hide it. This is exactly what I felt like doing when I was hurt in my heart and in my body. Hiding was the only way to cope. I knew.

It took decades for me to be able to express my true self. To hide physically or put a happy mask on my face when in public became second nature, until I went through a very severe depression.

The Healer Who Lived Down the Road

Every village had a healer, especially in Brittany, the Celtic region of France. Our local healer and his wife were about the only people my grandmother would visit regularly. They were kind to me and if a client walked in for a treatment, the healer didn't mind if I stayed and watched. I usually observed from the floor where I quietly sat beside their dog.

People would pay with vegetables or fruits from their garden, a bottle of wine or a chicken, never with money. The healer received his clients, like everyone else, in the room that served as both kitchen and living room. While the client sat at the kitchen table, he provided energy healing. His hands hovered above the afflicted part of the body, which he never touched. The only time I saw him lay his hands on someone was when a man, a miller, had dislocated his shoulder while carrying heavy sacks of grain. The healer rolled up a kitchen towel, placed it in the man's mouth, oiled the man's shoulder and put the bone back in its socket. I heard a loud grunt and that was it.

My grandmother asked the healer to help me only once, when I sprained my wrist. Without touching, he let his hands hover and twirl above my body. I was in a lot of pain but as soon as he put his hand above the swelling, it didn't hurt, it just felt warm. The pain was totally gone in a couple of days.

I was very fortunate to be able to observe how a traditional healer in a small sea village in Brittany worked. Decades later, it helped me to adopt this approach as I became a healer, and it taught me to always work in a very down-to-earth way. No need to make it complicated and expensive, just apply what you've learned, use your intuition, and stay away from any belief that isn't yours. It's a simple ability that all of us possess but few of us decide to develop.

I later had the good fortune to be trained by wonderful teachers, healers and shamans who always told me to learn the trade but find my own vocabulary and develop my own tools. That way I am able to remain true to myself and keep in close contact with my Spirit Guides

Once, when I was around seven or eight years old, we went to the healer's home, and as soon as we entered the house, his cat wouldn't stop walking back and forth rubbing my legs. It was a hot evening, and I was wearing shorts. She was constantly meowing, and I thought she wanted me to pick her up, but soon after she nestled on my lap, she screamed, and I felt her claws dig deep into my thighs. I screamed too. The healer came to my rescue and took her away, but not before I noticed what looked like a dark pocket come out of her rear end.

The next day, I came by to see how she was doing and saw her lying down with kittens. I asked if the black pocket I saw the night before was where her babies were. I didn't get a straight answer from the grown-ups—however, even though I was quite young, I had just learned how babies were born.

Until my late teens, I didn't have many opportunities to ask questions about the facts of life. The elementary and boarding school nuns were of course quite mum about the topic. This was an example of how Nature and animals taught me a lot when I was ready to understand.

Although life during my early years was full of challenges, I had the chance to live in a beautiful setting, perfect for the overactive imagination of a child. Our house and the garden with its wonders were perched on a rock surrounded by the beach; the sea, with the sound of the surf to lull me to far away shores; and the rhythm of the seasons with their rich fragrances to enjoy and their renewed treasures to discover.

In the evening, I loved to sit on the big rock a few steps down from our garden door. The remainder of the hot day used to linger there until very late into the night. In the evening, it was where I listened to the surf, the gentle lull of the waves against the rocks, and sometimes, in the distance, the humming of a boat. A soft breeze seemed to dispel the tension of the day. Scents from the sea blended with scents of the vegetation that grew on the rocks along the shore. My huge world was so peaceful. When the moon was not bright, the star-constellated sky joined the ocean at a line that was barely discernable. On full-moon nights, the shimmering path leading to the pale-yellow globe was inviting, but I would never have dared to follow it. Not because

I didn't know how to swim, but because as soon as darkness fell upon the water, the sea took on another dimension; there was something ominous about it. It became a world full of mystery and danger that would only be dispelled with the first rays of sunlight.

The ocean and the sky were the boundaries of my world. It was immense and yet, perched on the steps carved in the rock, I felt safe as soon as the night covered everything. It was as though the darkness wrapped me in a warm blanket in which I could hide my sorrows and feel warm in my heart. The serenity of the moment was mine to behold, and no one could take it away from me.

Years ago, I took my young son to "my" beach to share with him the magic of my childhood. I thought I probably wouldn't recognize what had been the magical world in which I could immerse myself. I knew all the nooks and crannies of the rocks, and most had meaning to me. Happily, all my favorite spots were still there: the treasure cove, the boat, the bathtub, the mountain. They just looked so much smaller. Of course, to be a few feet taller gave me a different perspective, but I also believed that my childhood's overactive imagination conferred to them status that my grown-up eyes could no longer see. The magic of those days was gone. Or was it? Later that day, I sat on a rock facing the sea and closed my eyes. The strong iodine scent, the call of the seagulls, the lapping of the water, and the faint breeze that brought relief to the irritating sizzling sun, all these familiar impressions suddenly engulfed me. It was so comforting to realize that, after all, nothing had changed. My mind's eye could still see the wonderful world I had created decades before.

CHAPTER 3

Teenage Hood

My father came back from Vietnam in June 1958, when I was nine years old. He was a stranger to me, but I was excited and thrilled to finally meet him. However, within a few hours, he had turned violent toward me and hit me. I remember watching his pale blue eyes narrow, and the sound of the violent slap he administered. I also remember very vividly that I stared at him right in the eyes and didn't cry. At that moment, I made the decision that that man would never be called papa (dad). Soon afterward, the decision was made to send me to an all-girls, Catholic boarding school near Paris. The school was part of a convent in a large building from the 17th century. It was very spacious and had a beautiful garden, but I didn't have the freedom to come and go as I pleased or escape when I needed to be alone.

The suppressed anger I carried as a child didn't disappear during teenage hood. I was very good at hiding the way I felt and never talked about it to anyone. From the outside, I was a very quiet, pleasant, and even funny girl. Inside, I was sometimes boiling with anger. Perhaps that's why, for someone who had led a very lonely life and learned to enjoy it, living with so many people without a break was very taxing at first. When I needed balm to soothe my hurts, there was no more immersion into "my" world by the beach, no more imaginary friends whom I could model according to my moods and needs, but instead only real-life, tangible girls to interact with. While having so many "sisters" was nice much of the time, it also became very crucial to find a way to insulate myself when I needed to. The sound of the surf, the bounty of the sea and the beach, the warmth of the forest and all its inhabitants, the flowers, and insects in the fields, everything that had sustained me during childhood was now gone. There was a lot of anger in me that I could control when I immersed myself in Nature. Now that I had left my seacoast village, I needed to find another way to cope if the need to isolate myself arose.

During early childhood, I didn't know what boredom was. Amazingly, later, when I went to boarding school and had to interact daily with so many other girls, I became very bored. I had friends and I wasn't bullied, but I found I wasn't interested in the things they were interested in. As long as I had the freedom to be alone and do what I wanted to, like read and draw, I was fine and enjoyed myself. I also learned over the years to create a public persona that was fun, positive, and energetic—a very tiring act that I found both natural and exhausting at the same time. I could only maintain that persona for a short period of time that grew longer as I aged. However, even today, although I truly enjoy being with people, I periodically need time alone to replenish my energy. That's when I don't answer the door or the phone. I may check my social media, but I don't interact. To this day, when I meet people, it's hard for them to believe that I'm introverted.

Gradually, I discovered that to put on a happy face and be positive in public helped me to feel that way deep inside. Seeing the reaction of others helps. It's like a mirror image of ourselves. Even on public transportation, I started providing smiles, especially to those I felt needed them the most. This trick wasn't always successful, but it empowered me when I felt it was received and helped. It changed my mood and elevated my spirit.

The first time I sat in front of a TV was when I was 15. On Thursday, our day off from school, the nuns allowed us to watch the weekly episode of the *Ivanhoe* series with Roger Moore. That was it. TV was turned on for the show and off right after it ended. There was a small library in the boarding school, and we were encouraged to read a lot. Books became my dearest friends; they could take me beyond the boundaries of the high walls behind which I led a very sheltered life. I could choose whatever location and century I wanted to visit, as well as the type of people I would like to live with for a few days. Reading also taught me a lot about family life and relationships.

However, being in contact with many girls is what first opened my eyes to what true family life was. Most girls would be gone for the weekend, home with their families, but during all those years, I rarely saw mine, even during the holidays. I never had a birthday cake or a Christmas celebration. I even spent a couple of Christmas holidays alone in the boarding school with the nuns. They were kind, but I wanted to experience Christmas like the other girls did. However, I can't complain since I also was very privileged. Starting at age 15, I never spent a Christmas or Easter holiday with my family, but I had the luxury of going to beautiful locations and visiting very interesting places when people still didn't travel much. I was sent to ski in Austria and the French Alps, and the summer months were spent by the sea, in the mountains, or abroad.

But I was longing to know what family life was like. I remember that some nights, I would silently cry myself to sleep because I was longing so much for someone to tuck me in and give me tenderness.

My Earthly Guides to Adulthood

My difficult-but-magical childhood had certainly molded me in a way that allowed me to naturally connect with the other side. The veil between the two worlds was very thin and sometimes even nonexistent. However, without a special way of growing into and through teenage hood, that connection might have faded away. There was a lot of anger in me that I could control during my childhood when I immersed myself in Nature. During my teen years, Art became its surrogate and helped me find and maintain peace in my heart.

I was very lucky to have been mentored by two remarkable older ladies. Both not only took extra time to guide my discovery and study of Art, they also were wonderful listeners. They responded to the questions I didn't dare to ask the nuns or talk about with other girls. I didn't have a mother or an aunt I could contact, but I could ask for guidance from them. I now believe they were sent to help me transition from childhood to adulthood.

Miss K. was not a nun. She came once a week to the boarding school to give me a private piano lesson. Soon, she encouraged me to attend classical music concerts in Paris's Chatelet Theater, which were offered almost every Sunday morning during the school year. I gladly followed her advice. Because I was only about 15, my father had to sign a release form that allowed me to leave the boarding school unaccompanied and go to Paris every Saturday or Sunday for the day. Since the performances were for an audience of mostly teenagers, each musical piece was introduced by a commentator who also talked about the life of the composer. I was fascinated as it transported me to places I had not gone before.

Miss K. became more than a music tutor, she also brought me what I was craving from an adult: attention, friendship, and recognition. I always looked forward to my weekly piano class with her, during which music was of course the main focus; but it also was a time when she would talk about Art and life in general. She helped me expand my mind outside the boundaries of the tall walls surrounding the boarding school. She was a mentor with whom I could talk about almost anything. I remained friends with her long after I left the boarding school, until the day she crossed over when she was almost 100 years old.

Since the Chatelet Theater where the Symphony Orchestra performed was only a few blocks away from the Louvre, and museums used to be free on Sundays, I soon started to spend the rest of the day at the Louvre. At first, not knowing the layout of the galleries, I wandered aimlessly. But after a few Sundays, I became so well acquainted with the layout of the floors that I could choose exactly where I wanted to go and what I wanted to see.

Paintings and sculptures were soon added to my other friends, the books and the music. Some art works would talk to me in such a manner that, when I would superimpose my own feelings on the lines, textures, and colors, magic would happen. It nourished my imagination and my need for the fantastic. I felt that my soul could soar more than when I sat in church. Like books, Art afforded me the opportunity to travel through time and visit places and people only visible in such a dimension. Scenes would come alive, and I would be taken to imaginary faraway places. I even had a boyfriend I would visit each time I went to the Louvre. After entering the main gallery upstairs, I would turn right into the second room, wink at *Mona Lisa* on the right, turn left and go straight to a very handsome and elegant man, *The Man with a Glove* by Titian. At this time of my budding womanhood, he was the embodiment of the man of my dreams.

The painting that moved me the most, though, was located further inside the main gallery. I could not view *The Old Man and a Young Boy* by Ghirlandaio without feeling overcome by strong emotion. More than once, I had to discretely dry a few tears. It was the most serene painting I had ever seen. So much love for the boy exudes from the decrepit old man. The beauty generated by love, not the face ravaged by time, is all the trusting eyes of the young boy can see. It was a feeling I had never felt directed towards me, and I longed to maybe someday experience it too.

The other teacher, Miss du C., was also not a nun. She taught literature and fine art and took me under her wing. She, at first, guided my readings. Some of the books she advised me to read were listed in the Catholic Index, which banned certain books. To get the list of what was forbidden was a gift to this rebel. It was thrilling for me to not follow it.

After spending many Sundays wandering through the Louvre, I felt the urge to draw some of the statues. I had great confidence I could talk with Miss du C. about it; she was already giving me so much guidance. Of course, she liked my idea and encouraged me to take a notebook and pencils to the Louvre. She even offered to look at what I had done. It had to remain a secret between us. We didn't think the nuns would approve of my nude sketches, even from statues.

Unlike today, the Louvre Museum wasn't very busy on Sunday afternoons, and it was easy for me to find a quiet spot where I could draw away from spying eyes. It felt like a forbidden game, and it delighted me. As I was progressing, Miss du C. even encouraged me to go to the Académie de la Grande Chaumière, where life-drawing sessions with nude models were offered.

Opened in 1904, it's an historical place that saw countless famous artists walk through its doors. Cezanne, Chagall, Delacroix, Gauguin, Miro, Modigliani, Manet, Matisse, Picasso, and others came to visit, work, or teach. As soon as I entered the building, I could feel I was entering another dimension. The spirits of so many great painters were still around, and I felt surrounded by so much powerful, friendly, and creative energy. Oh, I was extremely conscious that I knew very little and that I was just a budding artist. But I was craving to learn, and to be able to spend afternoons in such a renowned place made me feel special and happy.

I never talked to anyone there. I was very shy, and it was not a place for meeting people. During all the sessions, the silence was total, and I loved it. At the beginning of the afternoon, the models would pose for 45 minutes, then the posing time would become gradually shorter until it reached only five minutes at the end of the day. I always sat on the upper platform of the room, my back to the wall so no one could see what I was doing. But I could view very well below me so many great talents at work.

Of course, coming back to the boarding school, I had to be very careful to not get caught by the nuns. To spend some afternoons sketching nude models would have gotten me into a lot of trouble. However, Miss du C. and I were very careful and managed to keep my activities under the radar. I loved that little forbidden game.

Art would exalt, transport, and soothe my soul in ways that nothing else I knew could. Together with music and my old friends the books, it was enough to nourish my imagination, my need for the fantastic, and my soul. It helped me keep a balance between ugliness-hatred-anger and beauty-love-peace. When a child, I could take refuge in Nature; as a teenager I had painting, music, and literature to bring me solace.

I understood later from my Guides that Art was the best way to help me retain what Nature had taught me as a child. When we are in a creative state of mind, we can access the other side of the Veil with ease. The Veil disappears. We come close to our Guides. We are with them. Art allowed me to transition into adulthood without losing the connection with the Unseen.

I also don't think those two remarkable ladies entered my life by accident. I feel that my Spirit Guides placed them on my path to help my transition into adulthood. After all, like Nature, Art has the ability to stir very strong emotion, let the imagination flow unbridled, bring solace to a troubled soul, and sometimes bring humor when sadness weighs down the spirit. It's only decades later I understood these encounters and opportunities offered to me were Synchronicities to help me go through the growing pains of my teenage years.

My Other Haven

In my later teens, I also loved to go to Shakespeare and Co., a wonderful English bookstore and library across the river from Notre Dame de Paris

Cathedral. The bookstore was full of used and new books crammed on shelves from floor to ceiling, occupying any nooks and crannies available in the centuries-old building. The spirits of F. Scott Fitzgerald, Ernest Hemingway, Henry Miller, Anaïs Nin, etc., who often came to spend time there when they were in Paris, were still occupying the place.

At first, I would just wander around, basking in the special energy, grab a book and sit upstairs on one of the old couches. The beautiful atmosphere filled me with so much joy and peaceful excitement. I couldn't explain why, but it just felt right. All the books were (of course) in English and at that time I was still a bit limited in my understanding of the language, yet there was a lot I could absorb via osmosis, I guess. Sometimes, people would gather in the evening, share a large pasta dish, and read poetry. Although I couldn't understand all of it, I loved to sit there and listen to the voices and the sounds of words. Looking through the window, I could see Notre Dame de Paris nearby, all lit up.

On my way to the library, I would often stop, go inside the magnificent eight-century-old Cathedral, and sit there. The ambiance was always conducive to reflection—I didn't use the term meditation back then. The sound of the street was muffled, the light was soft and dim with sometimes a few rays of sunlight, and the scent of candles and incense permeated the church. It was always a place where I could find peace and where I could reflect and recharge. Sometimes, someone was playing the organ and it would make me fly to beautiful places. I cherished those exquisite moments.

When I was 17, several other youngsters invited me to spend Sunday afternoons with them. They all were very nice, and I was flattered to be asked to join them. They gathered in a private home with a large garden on the outskirts of Paris. It was very safe because the parents were always nearby. I tried hard to blend in, but I wasn't interested in the topics they discussed, and I was very bored. Ultimately, I went only two or three times. I missed my afternoons alone at the museum, letting not only my body but also my mind and soul wander through the long corridors among all the paintings, sculptures, and artifacts from times long gone. Some of the people would come out of the paintings and join me, or they would invite me into their world, take me for a stroll and show me details not visible to the naked eye. It was joyful and so interesting. I would always ride back to the boarding school full of new ideas for the week to come.

Those days spent with music and Fine Art helped me glide through teenage hood with ease. I was a loner but not anti-social. Weekdays in the boarding school with my friends were colored by the tone of my weekend outings, and if life seemed unfair at times, I always had the next Saturday or Sunday to look forward to. The theatre, the museum, the Art Academy, and many other special places in Paris became peaceful havens where I could replenish myself.

Looking back, I understand that Art was allowing me to continue to immerse myself in a different dimension, just like Nature when I was a young child. It helped me remain connected.

CHAPTER 4

Adulthood

In September 1966, I entered the *lycée Maurice Ravel* (a high school in Paris). Coming from a Catholic school and entering the secular system, I had to pass an exam to be accepted in the Literary/Philosophy section, which was where I wanted to be. I worked hard and succeeded. My dream was to become a journalist (foreign correspondent) and it would have been the first step in that direction. However, I was placed in the *section économique,* for those who wanted to become secretaries, not in the literary/philosophy section where I was supposed to be. I learned my father had changed my course of studies without having the decency to ask me or tell me! He thought I should become a secretary, not a journalist. He considered that profession too dangerous for a girl. I only found about it on the first day of school, when, very excited, I went to where I thought my classroom was. I was humiliated and totally devastated.

I was mad and refused to follow what my father wanted me to do. So, I reluctantly attended school for one year, but did not return the next fall. Instead, I escaped to London to work as an au pair and took English classes in the evening. After a few months, I decided to leave London and go to Cologne so I could further my German studies.

I worked there as an au pair for a German family until the May '68 student uprising in France forced me back to Paris sooner than I expected. I managed to get a seat on the last train crossing the border before France went into a total lockdown for several weeks.

Still very angry with my father, I had to keep my distance from him and get out of France again. He offered me money and a place to stay in one of his apartments in Paris, but the only thing I needed was my freedom. I got a summer job at the post office and bought a moped. I would have preferred a motorcycle, but it was too expensive. And I wasn't going to ask my dad to pay for it! I spent one week in the mechanic shop to learn how to take it entirely apart and build it back up. My goal was to be self-sufficient and not have to ask for help from men who, in return, might ask for favors I didn't want to give. My father always told me that he would have preferred a boy. I wanted to show him that a girl could be very tough and self-sufficient too.

Finally, I escaped and drove—alone—from Paris to Oslo. It took 10 days during which I camped at night wherever I could. In Oslo, I found a job right away and worked as a chambermaid for a few weeks, then in a restaurant as a cashier. It allowed me to save money to pay the tuition at a school I was interested in attending when I returned to Paris. I also took Norwegian classes in the evening and continued to study German and English.

My Modeling Career

Like many young girls, I looked at fashion pictures in magazines and had a secret desire to become a model. People also told me I should become a model, but while I thought it was a nice compliment, I also believed it would be ridiculous to try. I was too short and the models I saw in the magazines were all so beautiful.

This is me at a photoshoot in Paris.

When I was 22, I moved near Munich to live with my German boyfriend's family. I don't remember how modeling came into the conversation, but soon after I arrived, my boyfriend's sister said she knew the director of the best modeling school in Germany, and it happened to be in Munich. She offered to introduce me to this woman. Although I was very nervous, I accepted her proposal. Why not see what happened?

Frau Erika W., the owner of the modeling school, said she wanted to see modeling pictures of me and see how I walked on a runway and posed for pictures. She asked me to come back a couple of weeks later. I had no clue how to have fashion pictures made but my friend said she would contact a fashion photographer she knew. I met him, and he shot a series of beautiful photos of me and made professional cards.

I was getting extremely nervous. What was I thinking? I had never posed for magazines or walked on runways, and I didn't think I looked that beautiful. I spent many days trying to walk like a model and posed in front of a mirror imitating models in magazines.

Frau W. and I finally met again, and I was dumbfounded when she invited me to represent her school in a beauty contest between the best models from the other modeling schools in Germany. It was a black-tie gala she organized every year. I was shocked, thrilled and terribly nervous, but it was too late to go back. I could only graciously accept and move forward, although part of me just wanted to run away and hide. I had never taken a modeling class. How was I going to compete against 49 of the best models in the country?

The day of the competition was nerve-racking. The preliminary contest was in the morning. We were 50 women and only 15 of us were going to be selected for the final contest at the gala in the evening.

Ten judges were to select 15 of us, which was very intimidating for me. After all, the other women were trained models and gorgeous. I alternated between feeling elated to be given that chance and wanting to run away because I felt like a cheat with no right to be there. However, all went well. I was among the 15 women chosen for the evening contest. I still felt a bit out of place amid all those beautiful, long-legged women. However, one of the judges called me and told me to rest well and to be ready for the evening—I had a good chance of ending up in the top three finalists. I was thrilled and shocked at the same time.

If this were happening today, I would thank my Guides and ask them for strength to go through the evening. At that time, however, I had not yet realized that I was always protected and guided.

In the evening, when my turn came, I walked on stage in front of the long table where the judges were seated, then walked down the few steps leading to the long runway going through the casino. The venue was full, and everyone was wearing tuxedos and evening gowns. Everything went well until I passed by a couple of tables where people started booing and yelling words in English that I couldn't understand. I reached the end of the runway knowing I had to turn around and come back past the yelling tables again. I had no clue what was happening and felt miserable, but I had to keep going. I remember my smile freezing and my legs shaking but I made it back up to the top of the steps and passed in front of the judges again. When I reached the changing room, I was ready to collapse. Some of the other contestants were kind and helped me get into my evening gown. One of the women understood what the people at the yelling table said. She told me they were Americans, probably military officers stationed at U.S. bases located in Bavaria.

I soon realized what had happened. As I was preparing for the contest, it had been suggested that I use a stage name and make it more exotic than my French name. Since I had been born in Hanoi, we decided I should be presented as Li An Ho from Hanoi. But in early 1971, that was a mistake. I should have known better. Even though I wasn't following politics much, after all, there was a war in Vietnam in which America was involved.

This scary and traumatic episode left me with a grudge against Americans. I wasn't among the first three finalists and ended up as number five. I was so disappointed. The next morning, I woke up crying, but then, the phone rang. It was a proposal to go to Milan to be in a movie. I wasn't sure I wanted to do that and said I needed to think about it. *Something was telling me it wasn't safe to go there by myself.* Soon after, the phone rang again, this time for a modeling contract to participate in fashion shows for a minimum of two weeks a month. I had a meeting with the manager of the modeling agency the following day and a show was scheduled the day after.

I still wasn't sure I was tall enough, but the meeting went very well, and I signed the contract. It turned out my size was not an impediment, on the contrary. I was 22 but could easily look 15 years old, and since I was smaller than the other models, I could model teenage outfits. It was a lot of fun. We travelled all around Germany. Most of the clothes I wore on the runway were lovely. Since I was the smallest, the couturiers would design the most complicated pieces in my size because it took less work and material to make. I remember, for instance, a winter wedding dress covered with hand-sewn flowers made of mink and pearls.

I stayed with the company for about a year and then felt I had to move on. My dream had become reality, but I was ready to do something else. I had a wonderful time, and I also learned a lot about myself and how to behave in many situations. It was a great boost to my self-confidence.

I'm sure my Guides had a lot of fun helping me go through this amazing adventure, but I never thanked them then because, at that time, I had no clue about Synchronicities or how to make wishes become realities. I just followed my intuition. The only things I had to do were to accept the offers and dare to do it. The latter is what often makes many people balk and not take advantage of what's coming their way.

My First Husband

I returned to Paris to study and prepare for a career in international event management. In reality, I had two dreams. I dreamed of traveling to exotic places and visiting tribes in Borneo or the Amazon jungle. I also dreamed of marrying a wealthy man.

My first husband enabled me to achieve both.

Claude came into my life when I worked as a translator in a huge international industrial fair in Paris. His father, the CEO of a company exhibiting there, saw me and invited me for dinner so I could meet the business manager, his son Claude. Funny when a dad plays matchmaker.

Not only was Claude very wealthy, but he also had just returned from the Amazon, where he went to study medicinal plants with the indigenous Kayapo tribe. He told me he planned to go back, and it would be good if he were accompanied by a woman. Living with a tribe as a man alone wasn't ideal. Due to social taboos, there were many aspects of the tribe's society, such as the roles and responsibilities of women, that he was not able to study.

This was an opportunity I wasn't going to miss. Claude was thrilled when I told him I'd be very happy to accompany him. Everything was immediately put in motion. I started to study, joined the Société des Explorateurs (French Explorers Society) and prepared myself to go to the Amazon to live with the Yanomami tribe. We received a grant from the French Explorers Society, from Kodak, and directly from Prime Minister and future French President Jacques Chirac to study the medicinal properties of plants used by the indigenous people. The laboratory of ethnobotany in Paris was very interested in our study. I began receiving weekly guidance from some great explorers, including Joseph Grelier, who discovered the source of the Orinoco River and was one of my main mentors.

Société des Explorateurs Français. (French Explorer Society)
My future husband and I received 3 grants for our Amazon exploration.
The guest of Honor, Prime minister Jacques Chirac (future French
President), personally delivered the grants.

Before we married, Claude and I made two expeditions into the Amazon jungle (Roraima) in Brazil. Then we returned to France, married, and enjoyed a fascinating life together.

Recording during a ceremonial gathering of 5 Yanomami tribes.

Becoming a Dancer

Once when I was a little girl, I saw a ballet on stage. From that time forward, I always dreamed of becoming a dancer. I would dance in our garden or on the beach when no one was watching. When I went to boarding school at age nine, I asked to take ballet classes, but was always told that it was not a proper activity for a girl. My grandmother was the most adamant against it. She felt actresses and dancers were all "maintained" girls, which in her mind meant they were prostitutes.

I had already reached my mid-twenties by the time an opportunity was presented to me in the form of evening dance classes offered in the area where I lived. I thought I was already a bit too old, but nevertheless decided to try. After the first class, the instructor asked me how long I had been dancing. I told her it was my first class. She couldn't believe it and invited me to take some of the other classes she offered.

With my partner during a performance in Hawaii.

I was shocked when, after only three months, she asked me to take over a class that she taught weekly at a local high school. I must admit, I felt honored, but very scared to have to teach teenagers when I was just a beginner. Happily, it went much better than I anticipated, and subsequently my teacher suggested that I study at the École Supérieure d'études Chorégraphiques in Paris. She had graduated from that dance academy and offered to personally introduce me to the director. I wound up spending three years in a very strict school where I trained in ballet and contemporary dance.

After I graduated, my goal was to go to the States to spend a couple of years in Hawaii and New York to further develop my professional skills and to perform.

I had the good fortune to be able to join Betty Jones, whose contemporary dance company was in Honolulu. While sitting on the beautiful tropical beaches, it became clear I was craving true love. It took me back to when I was a child on the French coast, observing people on the beach and longing to be treated like the children playing and having fun with their parents. Nestled on the Hawaiian shores, I watched couples in love and wished I could experience that too. I realized that two of my wishes—for wealth and adventure—had come true easily. But I had forgotten to ask for the most crucial component in a long-term relationship: love. My husband and I were very good friends, but not in love. The lack of love started to weigh on me, and I realized I didn't want to continue on that path for the rest of my life.

Especially after I met Dave.

During the show "Kiss Me, Kate," my husband sang, and I danced.

I met my second husband-to-be on stage, during a show. I danced, and he sang. He was an Air Force officer, but he also had enough free time to be able to act at night. We fell in love, and it was everything I had been missing. Since I lived in Hawaii, away from my husband, we began spending more and more time together. Eventually, Dave proposed.

When he did, I had to think about it.

My answer was, "You need to understand, *we* need a wife. I don't like to cook, clean a house or iron." It made him laugh but I meant it. I don't like to do these things and I wanted to be clear right away.

Leaving my husband was a difficult decision. I would have to give up an exceptional lifestyle and a very desirable status. It would be difficult to get out of the marriage. My husband would feel very ashamed and never accept a divorce unless I took all the blame. It would also be very complicated. Divorce in France was legally very difficult. I flew from Honolulu to file for divorce in Montreal, where my husband was expanding his business and it was easier to obtain a divorce, then went back to live in Paris for a few months while waiting for the divorce to be final. To get out of the marriage as soon as possible, I turned down the generous alimony my lawyer told me I was entitled to and left France with nothing but my clothes, some books, my records (yes, we still had vinyl records then), my audiotapes—and my *freedom*. At last, we were divorced after eight years together. Looking back, I now consider those years very formative and positive.

Back in Honolulu, I finally joined Dave, the love of my life. We got married, and soon afterward, my husband was transferred to Washington, D.C. to work at the Pentagon. As I didn't know anything about the dance scene in that area, I called my cultural-attaché at the French Consulate to find out if he had any suggestions. He connected me with choreographer and teacher Maida Withers, who invited me to take one of the classes she taught at George Washington University. I took it and after class, she invited me to join her dance company.

I dreamed, I dared, I had faith, and my Guides were there to help me dance through life. So many Synchronicities helped me during this challenging but fascinating period.

It's important to never give up. Dreams might not come true when you expect them to happen. However, if the desire remains very strong, an offer might present itself when you least expect it. Even though I assumed I was already too old to become a dancer when the opportunity arose, I took the chance and stayed committed. Dance brought me to the U.S., where I met the man of my dreams, my second husband.

Life as a Wife (and Mother)

In 1986, I became a mother when our son, Kyle, was born. I worked as a Fashion and Image Consultant at the Academy of Fashion and Image in McLean, Virginia, and also trained models, taught poise, did color analysis, and more. Then, in 1988, Dave was transferred, and we moved to Seoul, South Korea. Then in 1990, we were assigned to Germany.

That was when I first realized something was not right.

CHAPTER 5

Depression

The move to Korea was the beginning of several stints living in different countries across Europe and Asia—the life of the wife of a military man. In normal circumstances, I would have loved the adventure, but my depression continued to worsen. After Germany, we moved to Italy, where painful situations piled on top of painful situations, but I kept my pain to myself. Then we moved to Japan, where I studied Japanese and Japanese Art History at the university. Since ancient Japanese art is related to myth and religion, I started to study Buddhism and spent a lot of time in Buddhist monasteries around Japan.

During this time, I discovered that my mother, who I had been told died in the 50s during the French war in Vietnam, was alive and living in Marseille, France.

As our move from Japan back to Seoul happened in early summer, our son and I decided to spend two months traveling to visit relatives in the States and in France. Of course, the idea was to meet my mother for the first time since she and I parted in 1950. I also was very eager to meet with my two younger half-sisters and half-brother.

While in Seoul, I received my bachelor's degree in English Literature with Honors and was invited by the honor society Phi Kappa Phi to become a member. I was a very proud, 50-year-old college graduate. But my depression lingered. From Seoul, we moved to Belgium, where our living situation was wonderful, but my pain persisted. I buried it in a flurry of activities. I organized an important fundraiser for our son's school: The International Dinner for Peace. I choreographed, I joined a political party, I taught Fashion and Image, Dave and I joined a chorus group, and I went to the gym every day. People thought I had it all—I had a handsome and successful husband, a talented son, a beautiful home. I was always dressed fashionably, and of course I was very busy with interesting projects. Little did they know that inside, I was dying. To the point where suicidal thoughts oftentimes crossed my mind.

I couldn't share this with anyone and had to hide my suffering from my child. I could only cry at night after he was asleep. I tried to be brave and do everything I could to occupy my time with a lot of activities that would, I thought, prevent me from falling too low. After all, depression was for sissies. I was a strong woman. I could face my anguish standing and let no one know about it. I had learned very early on to have a public persona, so it wasn't difficult to hide my pain. I was able to go on that way for a few years.

Then, a couple of years before my husband's retirement from the Military, we decided to buy a house in Clearwater, Florida, so we could move to that area when time came to leave Belgium. As it was where his parents lived and we visited them every year, we knew the area well and felt comfortable moving there. I decided to go spend one month in Clearwater, on my own, to explore and find the perfect home for us. It was much harder than I thought, and I wasn't certain that it really was what I wanted to do, but I eventually found a beautiful home with a large, covered pool.

However, the day I signed the purchase agreement, I had a very strong feeling I was doing the wrong thing. A part of me didn't want to live in a place that was so flat and so hot, but I tried to shrug it off, telling myself I was just nervous to make such a major decision. *My intuition was raising alarms, but I wasn't listening.* The evening of the contract signing, the realtor invited me to a celebratory dinner. She thought it was strange that I looked so sad. I just felt miserable.

I flew back to Brussels and tried to put the episode behind me. I even proudly showed pictures of our new home to everyone. A few days later, I had the opportunity to go to Rome and decided to take my son with me.

On our last day, as we were strolling through the Eternal City, suddenly something broke in me. I could not speak anymore. We were supposed to fly back to Brussels later that evening, and I still don't know how I managed to find the strength to do what was necessary to travel and go home. I suppose I still had to function for my son. My husband came back from his business trip the next day, and when he saw me, he immediately drove me to the emergency room.

It took me a long time to understand the reason why I broke down when in Rome. I had finally surrendered to my depression. And while the purchase of a house was adding to the gravity of my emotional imbalance, I believe what happened on our last day in Rome is the reason. Before returning to Brussels, I took my son to see the massive marble mask called the "Bocca della verità," or the "mouth of the truth." According to the legend, if a liar puts his hand in the mouth of the truth, it stays inside, and he can't get it out. When I put my hand in the mouth and it came back intact, I felt very uncomfortable. I knew deep inside that I was lying to myself and the whole world.

I think putting my hand in the Mouth of Truth was the catalyst that made me realize, at the unconscious level, that I was hiding the truth from myself, and it had to stop. The pain I hid so well was killing me. That's when I felt something break in me and all the pain that I kept bottled up for decades suddenly broke the dam, and it was an avalanche that buried me alive. That's when I suddenly was unable to speak.

I sank into a deep depression and felt suicide was the only way out. I planned three ways to kill myself and hid the means I needed to do so. If one way failed, I had two more options.

The day after we returned from Rome, when my husband came home from his business trip, I was catatonic. The only thing he could do was take me to the emergency room immediately.

I'm certain that my Guardian Angel helped me do what was needed to take my son safely back home and protected me so I wouldn't do anything to end my life.

Reconnecting with My Inner Child

I spent two weeks at the hospital, in the psychiatric ward, heavily drugged at first. But as I regained my faculties, I began to realize…

My Guardians were watching over me, as I had landed in the most unusual treatment center.

I spent two weeks in psychiatric intensive care and two and a half months in a mental health institute, and it was the best thing that could have happened to me. Therapy was provided not only via consultation with the psychiatrist and the care of the medical staff, but also via sport, meditation, art, and literature. For whatever reason, although I was in my early 50s, the medical staff decided to place me in the young adult section. Most of the patients there were in their 20s and 30s. It delighted me because the activities offered were all to my liking.

When I started to be able to walk, unaccompanied, to the Institute's little park, it felt so wonderful to be able to reconnect with Nature and to dance barefoot in the grass in the morning. One day, as I was sitting on a bench, reading, I heard light steps coming toward me. I looked around but couldn't see anyone until I lowered my eyes and saw an adorable young fox standing there, four feet away, staring at me. I looked at him and felt a jolt of energy crossing my entire body, but also warmth and joy. He slowly turned around and left in no hurry.

Was he a Messenger sent to remind me that Nature was still there for me to replenish the energy I needed?

Along with Nature, I could immerse myself in dance and Art via the daily classes offered at the Institute, including painting, drawing, clay modeling, music, and writing. I found again what made my younger years so special and was able to rekindle my love for the little girl waiting deep inside. It was such a joyful reunion.

With the return of the child came the ability to again see Signs and connect with the Universe

The cycle was complete, I was able to reunite with my inner child and understood the importance of never letting her go again.

For years, my pain surrounded me with a thick, dark veil that prevented light from coming through. In hindsight, even during the darkest periods, I received a lot of Synchronicities, warnings, and clear visions, but I was so consumed with trying to survive each day the best I could that I became impervious to the Signs and Messages from my Guides. I know I received and saw them because they are recorded in my diaries, but I didn't realize what they were or ignored the fact they were warning Signs or support Signs to guide me at that time.

CHAPTER 6

Becoming a Healer

In 2010, while on a several-week visit to Turkey, I became ill. Upon my return to Brussels, the sickness continued for almost five months. My doctors thought I might have caught something while traveling, but they couldn't determine what it was. Finally, after many tests, I was diagnosed with lung chlamydia and mononucleosis. Antibiotics didn't help, and I could barely function. My husband was on an extended mission in Pakistan, so I couldn't rely on him. I wanted to go to Brittany to see my healer, but I didn't have the strength to drive for nine hours by myself.

When my husband returned, he immediately drove me to see my healer, Mr. D. With his help, I was physically back to normal in five days. He also cleared some of my mental and emotional blockages. I cried during the first sessions, but I gradually felt the heavy weight on my chest get lighter until it was all gone. I have no idea how he did that, but it worked. I felt energetic again, physically, mentally, and emotionally. I had been unable to write or read for quite a while and had no interest in learning. Happily, I was now back to a place where the prospect of opening my mind to new things was exciting again.

Mr. D. had been known as a powerful healer for decades. During my relationship with him over the years, he had tested my healing abilities and suggested that I should follow his path. However, I didn't believe in myself and thought he was seeing something in me that I didn't have. I was also scared to go in that direction because of my early childhood. I had been intrigued by and excited about the paranormal from an early age. So often, things I couldn't understand happened to me, but I felt it was best to keep them to myself. To open up to the unknown and deal with and see things that others consider supernatural was spooking me.

Of course, the biggest deterrent was the fact that I had observed all those capabilities in my grandmother, and the ways I had seen her use them frightened me. I knew deep in my heart that some of her actions were wrong. For instance, she once showed me a photo of my grandfather. He was still alive, but I never had the opportunity to meet him, even though he didn't die until I was in my early twenties. My grandmother told me to look at him and started telling me horrible things about him. She took a needle and started to pierce his eyes. Then, with a pair of scissors, she started to cut his body into very small pieces, letting out a strange and scary laugh with each cut.

I knew she had some unusual capabilities. I remember very clearly when a small circus came to the village. We could hear a lion roaring and my grandmother told me to come along to see what was happening. The lion was lying down with his paws resting slightly between the bars of his cage, still roaring, when we arrived. My grandmother approached the cage and walked very close to the lion while staring at him in the eyes. She placed her hands on his paws and he immediately became quiet. The trainer was very impressed by what my grandmother had done…and so was I. But I was afraid I would become like her, so I resisted using my own abilities.

However, this time, something in me had shifted. I welcomed the idea of moving in a new direction, and the fear I had previously experienced was gone. Since Mr. D. had promised his wife that he would never teach others how to become healers, I pledged to him and to myself that I would search for a teacher. But I was thrilled to have guidance and support from someone who had already proven to me that he had unusual talents. I had known him for at least twenty years and had great trust and respect not only for his capabilities, but also for how he used them to help people around him.

As it happened so many times in my life, when something is supposed to be, there are new encounters and information coming my way. It's as if the stars are lining up to guide me onto the right path.

I was very excited, and although I realized there were tremendous amounts of research and training to do, I felt ready to concentrate my energy in that direction. I was at a place where I wanted to learn, explore, and discover again. My wonderful husband, of course, as always, was encouraging me to follow this new path. With great excitement, I started to dip into the pile of books I had bought.

Maybe I had to go through physical sickness and depression to acknowledge I was on the wrong path. Maybe they were necessary steps that guided me to Mr. D., the only person who could help me break away from that path and explore and embrace my potential as a healer.

Sadly, only five weeks later, my excitement and resolve to become a healer were already fading and my uncertainties were reappearing. That was when I went to the U.S. for a pre-Christmas visit with family and friends.

It was early December, and we were in Illinois visiting my husband's family. My friend W., who lived in Wisconsin near Lake Michigan, invited me up to go visit small towns around the Great Lakes that transformed themselves into Dickensian villages during the Christmas season. Once I arrived, however, a snowstorm was announced, forcing us to change plans. Instead, she offered me a Tarot card reading session in a small town nearby. She didn't know the medium well, but she heard he had a good reputation.

Arriving at his store, we were welcomed by a very tall man named Paris *(how strange!)* who looked intently into my eyes and greeted me with the words, "We already met!" I laughed and responded, "In another lifetime perhaps." He guided us into his office and asked my friend to sit in an armchair and me on the couch. Then he sat down in his own armchair facing me, closed his eyes and started to tell me my whole life. Not expecting any of what was happening, I was petrified and didn't move for the next hour and a half.

Everything he said about my past life was true—the way I approach life, meaningful events that no one knew about, and even some that I had forgotten but remembered as he was describing them. One thing that stood out, which he emphasized as important, was, "You've recently been contacted for the third time to become a healer, and you finally said yes. Don't fail to follow up like you did the first two times, when you were 39 and 49." I was dumbfounded! The promise I had made to myself five weeks earlier to train as a healer had indeed seemed less urgent lately.

It was such an unexpected turn of events for all of us. W. had requested a reading session for both of us, and the medium didn't know he would end up channeling me instead. It just happened. I'm glad W. sat with me through the whole session, because what the medium said was so unbelievable that I might have thought I misheard, misinterpreted, or even made up parts of the session. When we left, W. and I went straight to a nearby coffee shop so we could recapture and write down all that was said.

One month later, I was back in Europe visiting my sister in Paris. I asked her if she knew a place where I could buy a pendulum, which is a basic tool for a healer. She took me to a store called La Maison de la Radiesthesie (Radiesthesia) near the Madeleine. I never had gone to an esoteric store before and was fascinated by all the books and different artifacts I wasn't familiar with. On the counter were several pamphlets about different classes offered by a healer who called himself the Urban Shaman. I was intrigued, especially because I was very interested in every course he offered. They hadn't started yet, and *I innately felt he was the right person to take classes from.*

I sent him an email to tell him I was interested in all his classes. His first reaction? "Humph, a tourist!" He responded that we needed to talk by phone. Later he told me that he wanted to evaluate me energetically while on the phone to determine whether he could accept me or not.

I spent the next two years learning different healing modalities under his guidance, then another two years with other healers, psychics, mediums, color therapists, etc. to expand my knowledge. This was followed by five years during which I took more healing classes in France and many residential retreats at the Monroe Institute in Virginia to pursue my own exploration of human consciousness.

All the classes came into my life at the perfect time and in the right order. This illustrated the adage, "When the student is ready, the teachers appear."

Just when the promise I had made to develop my healing abilities seemed to devolve into wishful thinking, I had to come to the U.S., where, because of a snowstorm, I met a medium who channeled what my Guides needed to remind me: "Don't fail this time."

Looking back now, I know I was guided. Many new people came into my life, and everything happened, all in the right order and at the right time. Even though I was already in my fifties, I probably wouldn't have been ready when younger. I needed more maturity and wisdom to be able to go through the training. I would soon learn that with constant work, dedication and determination, anyone can learn these techniques. What I found more challenging was the complete personal transformation that, while needed, affected my entire being.

My life changed as soon as I started. It opened my eyes and my mind on so many different aspects of my life. It increased my awareness of being more than my physical body.

I find it interesting that I was reminded of my promise via a medium named "Paris" from a small town in Wisconsin, and it's in Paris that I started training to learn how to help others while walking in the light and staying away from darkness.

Part 2

As you hopefully noticed throughout Part 1, I have experienced Synchronicities throughout my entire life. On most of those occasions, I took action based on following my intuition—that innate faculty that we all have to gain knowledge without conscious analytic reasoning. However, once I started training as an energy healer, I began to better understand the origin of Signs, and how to receive and interpret them with more clarity and consistency.

In this part of the book, I will share stories of some of the biggest, most significant, or simply most interesting Synchronicities of my life. I also invite you to use several of these stories as inspiration to delve a bit into your own history. As you remember some of the "odd" events you experienced in the past, I encourage you to keep in mind that beyond our five physical basic senses, our intuition receives information broadcast to us by our Spirit Guides.

We receive this information via what I call the six "clair" senses, which feed this information to our intuition. While this news might come as a surprise, we constantly use at least one or more of these senses. Typically, a person is stronger in one, maybe two, of them.

Keep the descriptions below in mind as you read the stories in the following chapters. They could help you uncover your own Synchronicities if you choose to spend some time considering the "Points to Ponder" I have included along with some of the stories.

The Six Intuitive Senses

1. **Clairvoyance or clear sense of vision**

   The ability to "see" with your mind, not with your physical eyes. It's easy for you to "see" scenes in the past, present and future. It's a bit like watching a movie while closing your eyes. You have a lot of imagination and often have vivid dreams.

2. **Clairaudience or clear sense of hearing**

   The ability to "hear" with your mind, not with your physical ears. It's natural for you to communicate with plants and animals and "hear" them respond to you. You "hear" others communicate telepathically with you, or Messages that seem to be just for you, or the answer to a question you had.

3. **Clairsentience or clear sense of feeling**

   The ability to react to stimuli you receive from people or from your environment. It could be an unexpected physical sensation such as a sudden contraction in the stomach, a chill, or the hair rising on your arms. It could be a negative feeling as you enter a new location. It could be sensing that the spirit of someone who crossed over is in the room with you. The emotions of others can also strongly affect you and produce a reaction in your body.

4. **Claircognizance or clear sense of knowing**

   The ability to "know" something without any prior knowledge of where the information came from or how you got it. The insight comes out of nowhere but you're certain what you "know deep inside" is accurate.

5. **Clairalience or clear sense of smelling**

   The ability to "smell" odors that have no physical source. It could be the perfume of a long-deceased grandmother or some special scent from your childhood. It usually connects us to memories or indicates the presence of a deceased loved one.

This is one of the less common ways to receive information through Clair-senses.

6. **Clairgustance or clear sense of tasting**
    The ability to "taste" something that isn't there. The taste of certain foods that remind you of a deceased loved one could indicate the presence of that loved one is trying to communicate with you. This is also a less common way to receive information.

Help, Signs, and guidance appear in ways that aren't expected. It took me a long time, sometimes decades, to understand what a specific special encounter or event meant. Many of them seemed so odd at the time that they're still etched deeply into my memory. When I was younger, many of these strange happenings were very frequent and I never questioned why. But as I started to develop a sense of awareness about myself and gained more experience, I was able to better use what I understood were important Signs and be thankful for the Messages I received.

The following accounts of real-life events might trigger memories of similar situations that have happened to you, too. Some of these stories are from as far back as my early childhood.

To make these stories clearer to you, when appropriate, I indicate which type of intuitive sense was at work when they happened. I hope they will help you realize that you too have had, all along, the ability to see and act upon what you were shown.

I also hope that they will empower you to act upon what you have in mind and help it become reality, or maybe find an answer to a question.

These stories don't follow a chronological order but are instead categorized by topic. As I have lived in many countries and continents, they will take you to many places around the world. They also include some stories from other people I know who have also experienced Synchronicities.

You might be very surprised to discover you have quite a lot of interesting anecdotes that indicate that you too have seen Signs and been in connection with Spirit Guides. To put a name to the occurrences you experienced, refer to the descriptions of the six Clair-senses. Some of the events might fall under one (or more than one) of these categories.

I recommend that you keep a notebook and a pen handy during this segment of the book, so you can jot down what comes to your mind during the exercises, or at any other time. Or you could use the free Action Guide, which is available at www.winksfromabove.com/guide.

CHAPTER 7

Protection

When faced with a dangerous situation, it's not unusual that out of nowhere, an animal or a Sign makes us change our mind, an event might keep us away from harm, or we are "pushed" to react a certain way. I personally consider these appearances and happenings as interventions from my Guides or my Guardian Angel.

The Plane Crash

The day of my departure from Vietnam to France was set for June 11, 1950. Mrs. McBean, a British social worker, was to take care of me until our arrival in Paris. At the time, the Air France flight from Saigon to Paris stopped in Hanoi, Calcutta, and Bahrain, and the trip lasted three days. Just prior to the departure, my father was asked by French authorities if it were possible to postpone my flight until the next one. A military officer, an Army captain, had to return to France immediately due to his wife's sudden grave illness. My father agreed and gave him my spot. Two days later, on June 13th, that flight crashed under mysterious circumstances in the Persian Gulf. Because of my father's decision, my departure had been delayed until the 12th, and our plane safely landed on June 15th at Paris–Orly airport, where my grandmother and my aunt met me and took me to my new home in Brittany. Interestingly, on that same day I landed, a second Air France passenger plane, following the same route as the earlier two, also crashed mysteriously in almost the same location in the Persian Gulf.

It's an episode of my life that people have often commented on. As a little child, I couldn't understand the implications, except that I understood I had a Guardian Angel watching over me.

Point to Ponder

Have you ever experienced an unexpected, last-minute change in your schedule, and realized that you were lucky because it would have been a very bad experience or worse?

The Day I Drowned

I still vividly remember this day, which happened when I was about six years old. Our house and garden stood on a rocky promontory about 20 feet above the beach. Steps carved into the granite led directly to the beach, where I would spend a lot of time by myself. Beyond the sandy beach area, the rocks were always covered with seaweed and tended to be very slippery, but I didn't mind and loved to walk on that soft carpet, even when the tide was flowing in. It was fun to wade in the water, sometimes up to my neck.

That day, when I was walking in deep water, I probably lost my footing underwater and fell.

I don't know how many times I went under the water and came back up, but I still have the vision of what I saw. The wall and crenellated tower of our garden and the trees would become clearer, then gradually disappear. I remember going under several times. What is strange is that I don't remember fear overcoming me. My next vision is of a man, fully dressed in dark clothes, standing on the beach, and holding a little girl upside down. The scene appeared to be maybe 20 feet away from me. The next thing I was aware of was throwing up. When I opened my eyes, I was lying down on the sand and alone. No one was on the beach with me.

In the mid-1950s, beaches near our house were typically deserted most of the year. The people who lived in the coastal area where I grew up didn't know how to swim. Even though I spent a lot of time alone on the beach and in the water, I never learned this valuable skill until I was older. But it took decades before I felt comfortable in the water if my feet couldn't touch the bottom.

It's only later I realized that I probably had a NDE (near-death experience) and an OBE (out of body experience), during which I saw a man who was, I believe, my Guardian Angel.

The Stolen Wallet

One evening when I was in my late teens, I was with a friend in the Paris subway. It was a weekend and although late, it was still quite crowded. We stood at the end of a car holding ourselves to the central pole. When the metro rolled into my station, I put one hand on my tiny evening handbag and realized it was empty. Without knowing why, I instantly turned around, grabbed the arm of the first person turning her back to me, pushed her aside, did the same with the person facing her, then grabbed the arm of a third person turning away from me… and there was my wallet—in her hand! I grabbed it, rushed to the door that just opened, got off and stood there, like a dummy, holding my wallet tight, totally stunned by what happened. The doors closed and the subway slowly started to leave while the three thugs, as well as my friend, all stared at me, bewildered.

To this day, I can't understand how I was able to move so fast and push past two thugs and go straight to the person who had my wallet. I can only suppose that my Guide or my Guardian Angel helped me.

Point to Ponder

Have you ever acted spontaneously to something happening to you and your reaction was right, but you had no idea what prompted it?

The Stray Dog

Once, I accompanied my husband on a business trip to Romania. We stayed in a lovely spa-hotel in Constanza, near the Black Sea. It was nestled in a beautiful resort, which was usually very busy during the warmer months. But when we were there, in late October, the beach was empty and the area deserted. Although it felt a bit eerie, every day, I took a long walk along the Black Sea shores.

At that time in Romania, it was still very common for large numbers of stray dogs to roam in packs in populated areas. They were typically not dangerous, simply noisy when howling at night. The first day of beach walking, as I was leaving the hotel, a cute, good-sized dog came to join me. He wasn't begging, simply tagging along just like dogs did when I was a young child playing alone on the beach. He stayed with me until I returned from my trek and the hotel was in sight.

The next day, as I was starting on my walk, my new friend showed up again, out of nowhere. He happily trotted beside me through the small paths leading to the Black Sea and followed me as I was exploring the partially immersed rocks. He joined me every single day of my week-long stay except the day my husband had some time off and decided to join me. I saw my friend with another dog a bit further ahead, but "my" dog totally ignored me.

On the last day, as I was coming back from my final walk with my furry friend, I came across a couple of men who told me it was not safe for a woman to walk alone in that area.

That's when I understood that maybe this dog was sent by my Guardian Angel to protect me. How else could I explain that no matter what time I left for a walk, he would come out of nowhere and walk with me, then leave me near the hotel when I returned? The only day he didn't join me was when I took a walk with my husband.

Escaping Trouble in the Jungle

Before I married my first husband, we spent several months deep in the Amazonian jungle, far away from any civilization, studying the Yanomami tribe. Claude and I lived with the indigenous people in their large communal hut, which was built with palm leaves for the roof and walls made of vegetation and branches. A new communal hut doesn't have much of a problem with insects, but after a few years of wear, all kinds of creepy crawlies might fall off the walls or roof and onto you when you sleep. I was particularly careful at first, especially at night. However, after a few weeks spent living with the Yanomami, it became easy to not be as careful as when I first arrived.

One day, I needed something from my backpack. As I was getting ready to reach inside the bag, I had a strange sensation that made me recoil. I grabbed a flashlight to look inside, and I'm glad I did. A very large tarentula was hiding in there.

Walking through the jungle is *not* a stroll in the park. There are always so many unexpected challenges along the way, especially during the rainy season when the forest is flooded, and anything could be swimming around you. One day, as I was walking near the village, I approached a narrow creek that was probably no more than a couple feet deep and decided it was alright to cross over by carefully wading in the water. Suddenly, one of the tribesmen stopped me, and in response to my surprised look, he pointed toward the water, maybe 10 feet away on my left. Although I couldn't see anything, his actions led me to understand that piranhas were present, and it was very dangerous to go into the water. Knowing that they could strip a cow's flesh to the bone in minutes, I shivered at the idea of what could have happened had I stepped into the creek.

The Old Man in Venice

When we lived near Venice, Italy, I spent days bathing in the magic of the town, the source of inspiration for so many writers such as Hemingway and Ezra Pound. I loved to walk by myself through the narrow, meandering streets and stop to explore the architectural jewels, the historical landmarks, and the many churches with magnificent artworks. I always felt quite safe walking alone and never sensed I had to be very careful, except late at night, of course.

At first, I would ask for directions, but when the answer was invariably "sempre dritto," meaning "straight ahead," I understood the best way for me to learn the lay of the city (made up of 200 islands and 400 bridges) was to follow my intuition. I soon realized I could never be lost, only temporarily disoriented.

One day I decided to visit an area not far from the old arsenal, located at the far edge of the city and away from populated districts. As I was entering a deserted path lined with tall bushes and trees on one side and a long warehouse building on the other side, I felt someone gently take hold of my arm. It was a well-dressed old man who told me I wasn't in a very safe place. Still holding my arm, he guided me out of the area and back towards Saint Marco Square. I don't remember him leaving but suddenly he was gone. I had no time to thank him or say goodbye.

Of course, it could have been a good Samaritan wanting to help a young woman; however, there was something different about the man, something that I felt was odd. He said just a few words to convey his intention, but that was it. During the few minutes we walked together, I tried to have a conversation with him. Language wasn't the barrier, for I spoke enough Italian, but he simply nodded and remained silent, a faint smile on his kind, wrinkled face.

Escaping Trouble on the Beach

In 1979, my first husband and I had just arrived in the U.S. and were in Jacksonville, Florida, to meet a friend, another Frenchman who lived on Hilton Head Island. Because he wasn't picking us up until the next day, we decided to go to the beach.

Coming from France, we had never thought about the type of bathing suits Americans wore. My husband had brought a tiny swimsuit, like Frenchmen wore, and I only had a monokini (or the bottom part of a bikini), which was all I needed in France.

As we hit the beach, people were staring at us and making comments we couldn't hear. But looking at the facial expressions, we could tell they probably were not being very kind. We honestly had no clue as to why they looked shocked and offended. We thought the U.S. was an open-minded country. Then we looked around and noticed that all the women wore at least a two-piece bathing suit and men, well, it was very strange to see them wearing knee-length shorts as bathing suits. It seemed so uncomfortable.

Suddenly, the sky turned grey, and the wind picked up. People started to run away from the beach. We, too, gathered our belongings and ran away. We had never experienced such a storm. The wind was suddenly very strong and took my hat away. We reached the street and hid under an entryway just as the downpour hit. It was such a deluge, in no time, I had water almost up to my knees.

When our friend came to pick us up the following day, being French, he found the story quite amusing. He also informed us that we could have been arrested, or at least fined, for indecent exposure!

This story happened decades ago, and I spent a lot of time by the sea since then, but I never had to flee a beach because of a storm. Were our Guides and Angels watching over us and helping us avoid an embarrassing penalty for our ignorance?

The Almost-Robbery in Paris

During a trip to Paris, I was in a shoe store close to the Printemps department store. We were a bit low on euros but preferred to use cash over our credit cards, so my husband went to an ATM nearby. As he was finishing the transaction, someone rammed into his left side so hard that it spun him around so that he ended up standing with his back to the machine. He glanced to his left and saw the first man's accomplice, a tall man, with his hand already reaching for the card. My husband grabbed his wrist and wouldn't let go. Then the man who initially hit him approached him in a threatening manner. The situation was getting really bad.

Out of nowhere, a third man suddenly showed up. In a very calm manner, he got the attention of the attackers. He made sure my husband was all right and confirmed that they didn't have the money or the card. Then he told the men to leave immediately, or he would call the nearby police. As the thugs were walking away, the man again asked my husband if he had everything in hand. My husband checked the ATM for a last time to make sure his account was closed, and everything was in order. When he looked back up, the man who helped him was about 10 feet away, turning the corner into a side street. My husband ran to catch up with him to thank him. But no one was there. The man had vanished.

When my husband joined me at the shoe store, he was rather shaken by the incident that could have had serious consequences. For my part, of course, I was relieved that the scary situation had a happy ending and felt that it was my husband's Guardian Angel watching over him.

Later, Dave jokingly told me that it was probably my Guardian Angel making sure I got the money I needed to buy shoes. And yes, I found a good deal, two pairs of beautiful leather boots for the price of one. I still have them and think of the strange man who came out of nowhere to help my husband.

The Train Trip

This is one of those stories that is not about me. Instead, it happened to Clara, a beautiful, tall, young blond woman, when she took the commuter train to go back to Brussels. It was around 8:45 p.m. and not many people were traveling. The train pulled in and Clara stepped into the first carriage. It was totally empty and as she was tired, she thought she could close her eyes until the next stop in Brussels, 20 minutes away. But just before departure, four young men stepped in. She felt extremely uncomfortable, but it was too late for her to move to another compartment; one of the men was already blocking the door leading to the other part of the train. They surrounded her and started tossing their flip knives. One of them even kicked one of the top windows (the ones you can slide open) out.

Clara was terrified. There was no doubt in her mind what their intent was. She tried to look brave and talk to them, but she was starting to feel panicky. Then, suddenly, she heard "Good evening, tickets please!" It was a ticket inspector entering the compartment, which made the young man blocking the door move to the side. Clara jumped up, rapidly flashed her ticket at the inspector, scooted through the door, and moved to another part of the train. When the train pulled into the station in Brussels, policemen were there, waiting to intervene.

Even though she took that train often, Clara had never seen a ticket inspector at that time of day. Her Guardian Angel had stepped in to protect her.

Point to Ponder

When facing a potentially dangerous situation, have you ever had someone step in at the last minute to help you?

The Rattlesnakes

When my friend Naomi lived in Eastern Oregon in the high desert, she decided to look for a property to buy. She contacted a realtor she had already worked with. He told her he had a property she could look at, but unfortunately, he couldn't go with her. Instead, he gave her directions on how to get there. She thought that was a bit odd, but since it wasn't very far, she went ahead and drove to the place by herself.

She parked her car just before a path along a pond and decided to follow that path to go look at the property. She walked around to look at the trees and the lay of the land. On her way back, as she was walking beside the pond, she suddenly heard rattlesnakes. Three or four of them were blocking the way to her car. That's when she felt her body levitate straight up and over the rattlesnakes. She landed behind them and bolted for her car.

Shaking, Naomi was furious at the realtor for not warning her about the presence of snakes. Had she been bitten, with no one around for miles, she would have had to face the life-threatening situation all alone. As she calmed down, she was very grateful when she realized something extraordinary had just happened.

To this day, what remains deeply etched in Naomi's memory is the fact that she didn't initiate any motion or jump. It was more a sensation of being carried straight up and over the snakes. Naomi felt that it might have been the intervention of her Guardian Angel, and a clear Sign that it wasn't the right place to buy.

The Car Crash

When I was a model in Germany, I often traveled by car from city to city for runway shows. During one of the many rides to modeling gigs, our manager was driving, and I was seated beside him. We were chatting while he drove, fast as usual (it was Germany, after all). The traffic was busy but fluid, and he was an excellent driver. Suddenly, he turned abruptly, swerved the car into the emergency lane and jammed on the brakes till we stopped. We immediately heard crashing sounds. Cars were smashing into one another. I don't remember how many were affected but it was quite a few and, had we not left the road when we did, we would have been right there among the casualties. Our manager couldn't explain how and why he drove off the road. It just happened—he was as shocked as I was.

I realized our Guardian Angels were protecting us.

Point to Ponder

Have you ever suddenly, without any thought or understanding, taken a drastic, potentially dangerous action, only to find out subsequently that it was exactly the right thing to do?

Meeting my Mother

Towards the end of 1996, while living in Japan, I received a call from my father in Paris informing me that my mother had been found living in France. I was dumfounded. I always had been told that she had died during the 1950's War when Vietnam was still a French Colony. The last time I had seen her was when I was 15 months old, when I was put on the plane to France in 1950.

I decided to call her for New Year's Eve, and it was the strangest phone conversation I ever had. I had the feeling I was talking to a ghost, and

I didn't know if I should be happy or sad. I made the decision to go see her, with my son, the following summer.

As the train was entering the Marseille, France, station, I saw my mother and my two half-sisters, Jeanne and Marie, waiting on the pier. They had sent me pictures, so it wasn't difficult to recognize them. I was expecting to have a very strong experience, seeing the woman who gave me life for the first time. But there was nothing. I felt numb.

There was so much to catch up on to fill the gap of almost five decades. I knew so little about her and my family in Vietnam. Late at night, when my son was in bed, we sat in her very beautiful living room full of Asian artifacts and furniture. That's when she talked at length about her life. I discovered she was a very strong woman who always stood her ground, and despite spending time in Vietnamese refugee camps in the 50s had managed, on her own, to get to France and create a very good and prosperous life for herself. Quite admirable! It made me proud to be issued from such a fighter, a real warrior woman.

The first few nights as we sat by ourselves at the table and talked, something strange happened to me. Each time, I was surprised to find myself standing at the back of the room watching two women seated facing each other, on either side of a table. During these spontaneous OBEs (out-of-body experiences), I could see my back and my mother across from me talking sometimes with anger, sometimes with great melancholy. She never laughed, and many of her stories were heart-wrenching. I was fascinated and proud to have such a courageous and beautiful woman for a mother. Yet, I felt numb. There was no love, just great interest to discover who she was.

I believe it was a gift from my Guardians for me to have these spontaneous out-of-body experiences, so I could see the scene from outside myself like a movie, and not be involved emotionally. I had so much to process, I needed time to adjust to the new situation.

Point to Ponder

Have you ever experienced being separated from your body and sitting on the sideline as an observer rather than getting involved emotionally?

.

CHAPTER 8

Contact and Odd Encounters

*A few times in my life, I have come across interesting men whose
demeanor was unusual, but did not automatically understand the
meaning of those encounters. I say "men" because all the strange
encounters in this chapter involve men—for the most part, tall, slender,
olive-complexioned old men. The representation of the Angels or Guides
helping me are always males, or at least I sense their energy to be
such. It took me a while to understand the purpose of some of these
unexpected encounters, which were so strange that no matter how long
ago they occurred, they still remain very vivid in my mind.*

The Stranger in the Restaurant

One evening when I was in my early twenties and lived in Paris, a
girlfriend and I decided to have dinner together. As we entered
the restaurant, a man with South Asian features, impeccably dressed
in a dark suit, got up from the bar counter and walked straight to us.

He said he had an important message for me. Surprised, I looked at my girlfriend, who decided to follow the maître d' taking us to our reserved table.

The man asked me if I had a five Francs coin, which was a very large coin we used back then. I thought he needed the money to pay for his drink, but I was intrigued by what would come next and gave it to him. He asked me to place my hand, palm up, into his hand, then placed the coin into it and put his other hand on top of my hand. He then closed his eyes and started to tell me episodes of my life that I never had revealed to anyone, except to a couple of close friends. He went on to tell me about my near and distant future.

After he was finished, he gave me back the coin and, in response to my surprised look, explained he needed it to increase the contact and feel the energy between us. He said that he saw me enter the restaurant and knew right away that he had to pass on the message that was coming to him. Then we parted and he went back to join his friend at the bar counter. Quite shaken, I joined my girlfriend at the table where she was waiting for me.

What is strange is that almost everything he told me about my past had happened, and as far as the future was concerned, most of what he said did in fact happen throughout my life, and in the right order. For instance, he informed me that I wouldn't stay with my boyfriend because soon I was going to meet someone else, and it would revolve around travelling to faraway places. About a month later, I met Claude, who became my first husband.

Who was that man in the restaurant? Was he channeling for the Archangel Gabriel, the Messenger? Even though it happened over 50 years ago, the scene is still so fresh in my mind that it's like it happened yesterday.

Point to Ponder

Have you ever met a stranger who talked to you as if they knew you very well?

The Old Church in Athens

I was in Athens, Greece, accompanying my husband on one of his business trips. Each day, while he was working, I was invited to luncheons and organized visits around the city. It was lovely and everyone was very kind, but I was craving to be able to spend one day alone, to go where I pleased. However, to do so, for security reasons, I had to get permission from the admiral organizing the event. I was thrilled when it was decided that it was safe enough for me to go on my own.

As I was walking around the Acropolis hill, I came across a tiny church located below the path I was on. As the door was ajar, I decided to go in. I was greeted by a very tall, slender, wrinkled old man with an olive-grayish complexion. The room was small, with just a separation between the part of the room I was standing in and what seemed to be an altar, way at the back. There was something on the left partially blocking the view to the back. The man didn't say anything but indicated where I understood I should kneel, and he also pointed to something I should see in the direction of the altar. I knelt and looked at what he seemed to be indicating, but I couldn't really see anything special.

No one else was in the church, the room was very silent. I couldn't even hear the chitchat of the few people walking outside. Even though I couldn't understand what was so special about the altar, I felt very peaceful. I got up, smiled at the man, who nodded back, and left.

That evening, we had to attend an official dinner and I was seated in front of the director of the National Archeological Museum. She asked me about my day in Athens and I told her about my visit to the little church. Her face changed and there was a moment of silence. Then, with great seriousness, she told me that church was never opened, it had been closed for a very long time. I insisted that I went inside and described what I saw. She spoke in Greek to her sister seated beside her, then they both looked at me and asked when I was coming back to Greece. When I told them I didn't know, the director gave me her card and insisted that I should let her know when I did. She and her sister wanted to take me to Delphi.

Sadly, I never went back to Greece.

I keep wondering what was so important in the chapel that it had to be shown to me. I wish I could have understood the meaning of what the old man wanted me to see. The invitation I received that night to go to Delphi made it even more mysterious. When I finally asked my Spirit Guides, this is the response I received: "There was a lot you couldn't understand. To tell the Director of the National Archeological Museum *what happened, and to then be invited to go to Delphi with her was to make you realize you have power you don't accept but that others can see."*

The Man on the Adriatic Shore

When we lived in Italy, near Venice, we decided to spend a few days near a very quiet beach on the Veneto Gulf. One early evening as we sat on the beach, a young man came to join us. At that time of the day, the beach was deserted—yet we didn't see or hear him arrive. He seemed to have come out of nowhere.

I don't remember how the history of the area came into the conversation, but soon he was telling us in great detail about the life of the Celts who lived in the area more than 2000 years before. What struck me as strange was that when he talked about the Veneti tribe, he spoke as if he was one of them. The topic was extremely interesting. We had no idea that Celts had lived in the area. My husband, who is a history buff, was fascinated, and since my French family is from Brittany, the Celtic area of France, I too was captivated. The way the young man spoke was mesmerizing.

There was definitely something I couldn't define about him. The way he showed up, his voice, his impeccable and educated English, the stories… I felt like I was in a hypnotic state. It started getting dark, but I could see his face very clearly. There was something unusual about it, like a very faint shimmering of the contour. I don't remember how or when he left, just that I was hoping we would see him again.

Was I dreaming? No, my husband confirmed the young man really sat with us for a while, and he too felt the encounter was strange.

Who was that man? I always wondered if there was something to learn and we missed it.

Later I discovered there was a Celtic Veneti tribe in Italy which gave the name to Venice and also a Veneti tribe of Brittany, France, where my French side of the family is from, which gave the name to the city of Vannes. Maybe someday I'll find out more about that interesting piece of information.

The Ruins near Pompeii

A few years later, I went to Herculaneum, an ancient port town near Pompeii that was also covered by ashes in the volcano eruption in 79 AD. It had remained forgotten until the early 1700s.

I signed up for a guided tour and since it wasn't the tourist season, we were only a handful of visitors exploring the ancient town. After the tour was over, I enjoyed strolling by myself along the amazingly well-preserved streets, visualizing how life must have been then. Out of nowhere, an older man appeared. He seemed to be in his 60s and had grayish hair and an olive complexion. He offered to take me to places not shown to tourists during the guided tours. I should have known better than to agree to follow a stranger, but it felt right. And after all, even though the site wasn't busy, it wasn't deserted.

The stranger took me to places that could only be reached by following special passageways. We went through the area of the gymnasium that had been partially excavated and many other places closed to the public. He pointed to attract my attention to some important details, but I must admit that at the time, even though the whole encounter felt a bit strange, I didn't realize how special it was. It was only much later that I understood all that he was trying to share with me.

I went back another day with my husband. I thought I would find the man and ask him to take us on a private tour. I looked everywhere, but he was nowhere to be seen.

Who was that man? Why did he take me to so many interesting places not opened to the public? What was there for me to learn and what did I miss? Much later, I came to understand from my Guide that I had "treasures still buried deep inside me," and that I had to excavate and search for the wealth of information that still needed to come to the surface.

The Old Taxi Driver in Paris

I had just completed a weekend seminar on intuition and developing Extra Sensory Perception (ESP) and walked to a taxi to go to the train station. The driver had the same look as my other "mystery men"—he was very tall and slender, with a wrinkled face and an olive-grayish complexion. I immediately noticed that while he looked very old, he didn't move like an old man. He got out of the car with great ease and swiftly lifted my heavy suitcase.

When I told him where I was going, he apologized and said there was an accident on the way, and it would be better to take a longer but faster way to drive to the station. I thought he was trying to make more money out of the ride, but I didn't say anything. I was feeling very mellow after two days spent meditating and working on techniques to develop my ESP. Shortly after I got in the car, the driver started to talk to me in a very elegant and educated voice about the importance of being one with the Universe. It was very odd to hear this man, a taxi driver, talk about the main topic of my just-finished weekend seminar, particularly when I had not initiated the conversation. What he was saying was very profound and beautiful and his vocabulary was exquisite. I wish I had thought of recording him, but I was a bit worried because he kept looking at me directly via the rear-view mirror more than he paid attention to the heavy traffic. I felt uneasy yet calm at the same time. It was a fascinating ride that took at least twice the time it normally takes.

When he dropped me off at the train station, to my surprise, the fare was much lower than usual. He then shook my hand while staring deeply into my eyes and said, "We'll meet again!"

It was a very powerful moment. It's not only my hand that was shaken, but also my whole being. I realized that something special had just happened. The shaman I was studying with told me it probably was one of my Guides appearing to emphasize and validate what I had just learned during the weekend.

The Train from Paris to Nantes

Our overnight flight from Washington, D.C. had landed early in the morning at Charles de Gaulle airport near Paris. I was waiting at the Roissy train station to board a high-speed train for the two-and-a-half-hour ride to the town where my father lived. As I was waiting on the platform at the spot where my first-class car would be, an older man in a white linen suit and a white hat showed me his ticket and asked me if he was in the right place. I said "Yes," and he stepped away. He was quite dapper in his white outfit that reminded me of older gentlemen in Central America. However, he seemed a bit out of place in Paris at the end of September.

The train arrived, I climbed in and proceeded to search for my seat on the lower level of the double-decker car. I realized it was on the upper deck and walked upstairs, and as soon as I entered, I noticed that no one was there but the gentleman in white. I looked for my seat and discovered it was the one right next to him. As I had the window seat, he stood up to let me in. Maybe a couple more passengers walked in, but that was it.

I was very tired after the long overnight flight and wasn't in the mood to be very sociable. I placed my bottle of water and the book I was reading with my train ticket tucked into it on the table in front of me. I was getting ready to relax and enjoy the ride.

The man pointed at the book and asked: "You speak English?" I told him yes, I'm French, but I live in Virginia. "I live there too," he said. As we spoke, I discovered that he not only knew the town I lived in quite well, but also some of my acquaintances and places that I love to visit. I was surprised when I commented on the expansion of a beautiful Tibetan monastery I had recently visited in the mountains, and he explained that he helped design the newest building in the complex.

Then he asked me if we could meditate together. As soon as I closed my eyes, it was very peaceful. At one point, I saw a black lightning bolt against a beautiful deep red background. Nothing scary or ominous, it was just strange.

After we opened our eyes, he was very interested to know if I saw and felt anything special. I told him about the lightning bolt and felt it was related to his heart. He smiled, thanked me, and said that it was helping him a lot.

When I found out he was going to get off at a town 30 minutes before my destination, I asked him what he was planning to do there. He replied that he was going to stay and help in a monastery for a couple of months.

As he was saying goodbye, he thanked me again and stressed how much our meditating together had helped him. To my surprised look, he said, "You wouldn't understand."

He left and I was puzzled by this strange encounter. Later I understood it meant that "it was to make me understand I needed to believe in my own power."

Gabriel in a Paris Restaurant

I was in Paris to attend one of my first trainings on energy healing and decided to go to Chartier for lunch. Years ago, the Chartier restaurant was very popular. It was one of the brasseries that hadn't lost its turn-of-the-century early 1900's style. The original decor and the obsequious waiters who would greet patrons in a style from another era were very appealing to many people. During lunch time, the line to enter was always long and often spilled out onto the sidewalk.

As I approached, the line was, as usual, very long. When I finally entered the restaurant, I wasn't surprised to be assigned a seat at a table for two where a gentleman was already seated and halfway through his meal. After the initial greeting, I don't know how the conversation shifted to healing, but he certainly had a lot of interesting stories to tell about traditional healers in Corsica, where he said he was from. He provided me with encouragement when I told him I was starting on that path. I found it strange that this topic I wasn't yet comfortable discussing with anyone, came up so soon in a conversation with a total stranger.

He finished his meal while I was still eating my steak-frites and salad (French fast food). He apologized and said he had to go—he was a businessman and was in Paris to attend a convention. He called the waiter and asked him to add my meal to his bill. I was shocked but grateful. When he got up to leave, I asked his name. With a grin he said, "Gabriel."

Although I was at the table for another 15-20 minutes and the waiting line was still long, no one else was assigned to sit with me. The next day, when I saw the shaman I was studying with, he smiled and told me it was probably a Messenger who came to encourage me on my path. Was he Archangel Gabriel, the Messenger?

CHAPTER 9

Knowing

There are times when we "know," but our brain is quick to squelch the input because it doesn't always seem to make sense. This clear sense of knowing is called Claircognizance.

Children take this kind of information as it comes and don't filter it as grownups do. Our son was like this, and when he was very little, he frequently had insights that surprised us. Often, they were about death. The following stories happened at a time when none of us had mobile phones and social media wasn't yet part of our lives. Hence, our son had no way to be informed about the incidents he "knew" about.

It was early August 1997 and we had just arrived in Paris. One afternoon, I decided to take my son on a boat ride on the Seine. We sat on the top deck admiring the magnificent monuments. As we were passing the Louvre, my son suddenly asked me if the oldest lady in France had died. I was surprised, for I didn't even realize he knew about Jeanne Calment, who at the age of 122 was the oldest person in the world. I told him I didn't know. We had been travelling for many days and I didn't pay attention to the news.

That evening, we had dinner with my sister and my nephews. During the conversation, someone mentioned that Jeanne Calment has died earlier in the day.

What made him ask the question earlier that day?

When we lived in South Korea, I would only get my mail when my husband brought it home with him after work. Since I was busy helping our son, who was then 11, with his homework and preparing dinner, I would usually read my mail after he went to bed. That night, the letter I received from France had terrible news. My cousin, still a young man, had fallen down a staircase, broken his neck and died immediately.

As my husband was working late, I didn't break the news to him that night, and I didn't speak to anyone about it. The next morning, during breakfast, I asked my son, "Do you remember Cousin Patrick?" "Yes, he is dead," was his answer. I was shocked. "How do you know that?" I asked. He answered, "I just know."

He couldn't explain why he knew.

A few years later when we lived in Brussels, one morning during breakfast I reminded my son to hurry home after school for his piano lesson. He said he didn't think our piano teacher would come because of a death. I asked him what he meant by that, but he just shrugged.

In the afternoon, the teacher called to let me know he couldn't come. His dog had gotten very sick, and he had to take her to the vet where she had to be put to sleep.

How could our son know a death was imminent? It was early morning, before the dog was taken to the vet.

These three incidents indicated to me that our son was connected and able to receive Messages from Above. They came as information that he couldn't explain.

Point to Ponder

Have you ever had a hunch you couldn't explain but that later proved to be true?

CHAPTER 10

Communication and Unexpected Connections

All around us, there is so much we miss when we don't pay attention or can't understand. Departed family members and loved ones are not the only ones who try to communicate with us.

My sisters Jeanne and Marie from Marseille contacted me in Brussels to let me know our mother was fading fast. If I wanted to see her alive, I should come right away. Anne-Marie, my sister in Paris, received the same message and she and I arrived by train at almost the same time. Friends were waiting for us at the station and took us straight to the hospital. Maybe ten family members were already there, surrounding the bed. Our mother was hooked to a ventilator and couldn't talk very well because of the mask, but she was still alert.

Although she already had been given a lot of morphine, she seemed in great pain and moved her hand to hold the upper side of her left breast. The pain seemed so intense we called the nurses. Two or three came running in and checked everything but they couldn't find what was wrong. At one point, my niece and myself were the only ones left with her in the room.

To see my mother grimacing in pain, I knew I had to do something. Until then, I hadn't shared the fact I was training to become a healer. After all, I didn't know my mother too well. I was 48 when I first met her, my two half-sisters and half-brother for the first time. But for some reason, this time I didn't hesitate to do what was necessary. I placed my right hand just above the area where she had pain, closed my eyes and…the pain hit me in exactly the same place. It was excruciating. I looked at my mother and made a gesture with my head to ask how she was doing. She looked at me and smiled. Obviously, the pain was gone from her, but not from me. I went to the sink nearby and rinsed my hands and forearms to remove the negative energy.

My niece saw everything and asked if I had worked on my mother. Of all the family members, she was the only one who could understand what I had just done. Her boyfriend is an osteopath, and she is a pharmacist.

The following morning, my mother's death was imminent. However, we were hoping for our brother Charly, who was arriving from Noumea, New Caledonia the next day, to be able to see her alive. As Anne-Marie and I were getting ready to leave to spend the day with her at the hospital, we got a call to inform us she had just passed away in her sleep, around 9:00 a.m. When we arrived, our sisters Marie and Jeanne were waiting for us. Mother's bed had been wheeled into another room and she was left untouched, still in the position she was in when she died. Since our mother's legs were apart under the blanket, Anne-Marie helped me to put them back together. Her body was clammy and still warm, and her face was relaxed. She obviously died during her sleep. After my sisters left the room, I had the privilege to be left alone with her for 15 to 20 minutes before the nurses came in to prepare her. I sat on the bed, and it struck me how strange the date was. It was my birthday. Tears started streaming down my cheeks as

I told my mother, "62 years ago, you were in a hospital bed in Hanoi ready for me to take my first breath. Today, you are in a hospital bed in Marseille with me sitting beside you and you just gave your last breath. The cycle of life is complete."

I realized that maybe the nurses would think it wasn't proper to sit beside a corpse on the bed. So, I sat on a stool beside the bed, closed my eyes and started to meditate. *I felt my mother was still in the room. The energy was peaceful and beautiful.*

I have to say that my mother was almost a stranger, since I was sent to France when I was 15 months old and never saw her again until I was 48 years old. After that, I met with her only four more times before she died. So, to me, she was someone I didn't know well and never had the opportunity to develop a normal bond with. I tried to call her "maman" (mommy), but it felt too strange, and the word never left my lips. I also was never able to use the familiar form of "you" ("tu" in French) when I talked with her but could only address her as "thou," the very formal term.

However, our story doesn't end there. Throughout the following year, there were many moments I felt she was close by and helping me.

It started when she was still alive, in her hospital room, when I tried to relieve her of the pain she was experiencing and felt that pain immediately after removing it from her. The shaman I was studying with explained to me that my mother wanted to give me proof that I was on the right path as a healer. Since the niece who witnessed the scene told other family members about me, I ended up successfully helping them with various pains and aches during my stay. It was quite a boost to my still-hesitant approach to healing.

Several times during the next few months, shamans and intuitive people would tell me they could "see" a white horse right behind me. It was mindboggling to me that people who barely knew me and didn't know each other would "see" the same thing. I also saw horses everywhere.

My siblings gave me a small, round Asian table my mother had beside her bed. In her house, it had been covered by the large base of a lamp, but with the lamp removed I saw the carving of two horses running side by side.

I love horses but I'm not obsessed by them, so it was really puzzling me. A year later, I was traveling with my brother to attend our mother's death anniversary Buddhist celebration and told him about the horse constantly appearing in my life since our mother crossed over. He laughed and told me that her Chinese zodiac sign was the Horse. I had believed until then that her sign was the Tiger.

I began to learn that Ancestors, departed family members and friends can also be called upon if we need help. Many of them may become part of our Spirit Guides "team." Suddenly, the presence of the ancestors' altar in every Far Eastern home and the general veneration of ancestors started to make sense to me. Although my mother was almost a stranger to me in this life, she manifested herself after death in ways to show her support. Since then, I have seen her during an OBE, and it felt so strange but pleasant when she hugged me. I never experienced that when she was here in person.

Point to Ponder

Have you ever felt the presence of a departed loved one near you? Have you ever caught yourself "talking" to a departed loved one?

My Father, the Day He Died

In early December 2018, I had a very unusual night. I couldn't breathe easily. I felt like there was something heavy on my chest and I kept tossing and turning.

My dad was very sick, and I was worried I might have to go to France during the holiday season. It's never fun to fly during that time of the year, and that made me angry. Angry at the situation, angry at my dad, and angry at myself for feeling that way. It wasn't his fault, of course, but it was bringing up all kinds of negative feelings from the past. We never had a close relationship and even didn't speak to each other for many years. Only when my son was born did I make an effort to renew contact with him.

When I first found out he was very sick, I went to France to spend two weeks with him, then returned to the U.S. After several subsequent agonizing and uncertain weeks spent waiting, I started to think that if he died right then, maybe I shouldn't go back, but could instead hire my cousin, who is a maître d', to organize a reception with a buffet and drinks after the funeral.

I was so upset that I couldn't sleep at all.

My husband had a great suggestion. If my dad were to pass, why couldn't I delay my trip to Nantes until after the holidays and then host a celebration of life for him? We had done that for his mother. I didn't know whether it would be appropriate in France, but it was worth asking my cousin for his advice. Then my husband massaged my head and shoulders, and only then was I able to get some sleep.

I woke up a couple of hours later feeling very calm about the decision to miss the funeral and offer to organize and pay for a reception right after the ceremony, then organize a celebration of life gathering for later in the spring. I would call my cousin and my dad's wife later that morning to talk about the idea.

The previous year, in the living room, I had created a special Christmas display for the alcove above the fireplace. It had three angels, Christmas foliage, flowers, and a beautifully animated light effect. I was very pleased with the result and wanted to re-create it that year.

Now, normally I'm very organized and I always keep detailed records of Christmas decorations/scenes I create. But this time, I couldn't find any pictures or notes that showed me how I did it. Even some decorative elements were missing. This was truly bizarre. I was drawing a blank, and it was very frustrating. I felt my best hope was to start from scratch and ran to the store to get new greenery, flowers, and lights.

It didn't take long to find exactly what seemed right and I came back ready to put everything together. It took me most of the afternoon, but I was very happy with the result. It was beautiful even though it was different from the year before.

Later that day, just as I was ready to call my cousin, the phone rang. It was my cousin calling me to let me know my dad had just passed away. Since France is six hours ahead of the U.S., he crossed over when I was creating the Christmas display.

And the story doesn't end there…

The following morning, I walked downstairs to get coffee—but first, I went to the window to see if the heavy snow that had been forecast had started to fall. I was concerned because, a few days before, a medium had warned me about a coming life-changing event that would somehow be related to snow. It upset me tremendously. Our son spent each day driving on very dangerous roads through the mountains, and I was scared something bad would happen to him. However, another medium thought the event wasn't related to my son, but to my father.

A few flakes were already twirling, and it was very pretty and mesmerizing. On my way to the kitchen, the display I had made the day before caught my eye. I looked at it and was stunned to see what I had created. The greenery I placed behind the angel made its wings appear bigger. Even without the animated lights, it looked stunning and magical. It was so strange; I felt I had been guided to place the foliage, the flowers, and the lights in a way I had no control over. Suddenly, my whole body started to shake, and I went into a powerful trance. Tears began to stream down my face, and I heard the voice of my father say, "I'm all right, I'm sorry," over and over.

I was stunned. My relationship with my father had never been very good. When I tried to get closer to him when my son was born to make sure he got to know his grandson, even that didn't work out as well as I expected. To hear him apologize to me was so strange. He never did so when he was still alive. But it was him, my dad, there was no doubt. It was unmistakably his voice.

My husband witnessed what happened and told me I was very pale, shaking, tears running down my face and that it probably lasted 10 minutes. When I came back to normal, I was so exhausted that I went back to bed and slept very deeply.

Many months later, I learned that I had experienced a moment of Clairaudience. My Guides revealed more details about what happened. *"Yes, your father spoke with you. He was still in transition; therefore, he was limited in how much he could express himself, but he wanted to let you know that he loves you and was sorry for not being the father you deserved. Take it as a learning experience. Your lack of family love and support helped you to become the compassionate person you are. Suffering in your heart can open it to love others because you understand their pain. One of the ways to reach that level is through experience, sometimes a very painful experience.*

Your father has now fully transitioned and has found friends and family members. You can contact him if you want. He will provide the help you need. He is now part of your team of helpers and will remain there forever. Your mother is there too, and she is also ready to provide assistance."

The special alcove with angels is now a holiday shrine not only for my dad, but also for all my family's and friends' ancestors. It's a beautiful place to meditate and connect with them during the holiday season. Sometimes, in the evening, my husband and I sit in front of it to reminisce about the time when those we loved were still among us.

The House in Manoa Valley

When I lived in Honolulu, I went several times to visit friends in Manoa Valley, a beautiful area close to the mountains. I must admit that I never felt comfortable going there. Each time I crossed the threshold of the house, a shiver ran down my spine. It was very unpleasant but disappeared soon after I went in, and no other spot in the house would bring this type of reaction. I had a little idea of what it could be but at that time, I was still unwilling to talk about those types of feelings. How could I explain to people that I "felt" something bad happened in their house?

Then one day, I couldn't wait any longer and asked if something strange ever happened there. "Yes," someone said, "a previous tenant hung himself."

I wasn't surprised to hear something dramatic had occurred in the house, but at that time, it didn't go any further. Decades later, when I trained as a healer, I learned that I was experiencing Clairsentience when I entered that house, and that those hunches were right. Today, I would probably burn a candle or incense and pray to assuage the suffering of the soul.

Point to Ponder

Have you ever felt some uneasiness you could not explain when entering a house or other location?

The Phone Call

My sister Anne-Marie was still in bed one morning when she heard her husband call her with a sense of urgency. She jumped out of bed and ran to the living room. Her oldest son, his wife, and their young daughter were staying with them, and her son came out of his room and said he heard his dad scream. My sister asked her daughter-in-

COMMUNICATION AND UNEXPECTED CONNECTIONS

law, who was making coffee in the kitchen, if she had heard or seen her husband, to which she responded, "No." Her granddaughter was watching a cartoon on the TV in the living room, and she too said she hadn't seen her grandpa.

Suddenly, my sister heard a weird snorting sound near the bay window leading to the terrace. Her husband was slumped on the ground having a heart attack maybe 12 feet away from his daughter-in-law and granddaughter, who didn't hear anything. How odd was that? He died soon after. To this day, my sister and her son are very puzzled by what happened two decades ago.

Then, two days after this incident, my sister's youngest son came to have breakfast with her. As they were talking about the deceased, the son mentioned that while taking his shower, he wished so much to know if his dad was okay on the other side. Almost immediately, the phone rang, and it went straight to the answering machine. Instead of a voice, there was only beautiful classical music—the type that his father loved. My sister immediately got up and checked the phone. She saw that the call came from an unknown number and that it was indeed a piece of classical music, not some kind of advertisement.

Right away, my nephew understood that it was his dad answering his question.

What happened? Was my sister's husband reaching across the veil to tell his son he was, in fact, okay on the other side? This was another clear instance of Clairaudience.

Point to Ponder

Have you ever received a sign from a deceased loved one or felt his or her presence? For many people, the connection isn't interrupted by death. It continues at another level.

119

Connections with the Animal World

While exiting a restaurant, I heard a crashing sound against a window. I checked to see what it was and saw a woodpecker laying on the ground. It had probably rammed into a window and was knocked out. I carefully picked it up and held it in my hand to check if it broke its neck. It opened its eyes, slowly came back to life, straightened itself and stood up in my hand, turning its head to look at me. It didn't seem frightened.

I was with several family members, and everybody was waiting to go home. I tried several times to lift the bird so I could put it on the low branch of a tree, but it was clinging to my fingers with its feet and didn't want to let go. It took at least 30 minutes before it agreed to release my hand and be placed on a tree. What a beautiful bird, and what a privilege to have been able to hold it. What's funny is that on that day, I was wearing a black and white patterned jacket that matched the bird's beautiful markings.

However, again, the story doesn't end there.

Soon after we got home, as my husband was sitting outside on our deck, a woodpecker perched on the nearest branch of a tree facing the terrace. He started singing while looking at my husband. We have many birds in our backyard who delight us with their beautiful songs, however, they don't usually sing while staring at us. This bird seemed to be deliberately looking at my husband while singing. My husband called me, and I stood there for a few minutes until the bird stopped singing and left.

What happened? Was the bird a Messenger thanking me for helping one of his kind? We found this lovely event quite unusual but heartwarming. I helped the bird, and I received a thank you! I'm still very touched.

When we bought our home in Brussels, there were already several bird nests in our courtyard. One was a thrush nest. The birds loved to rebuild it in our thick ivy each year during nesting season. It was such a privilege to hear their beautiful melodies every morning before sunrise.

One late spring afternoon, I noticed one of their new baby birds standing in the middle of our courtyard. I thought the parents must be nearby searching for food. It's always so adorable to see the mother and father birds looking around the ground for something to eat with the little ones following them. A little while later, the cute roly-poly chick was still standing in the same spot in the middle of the courtyard. It worried me because the year before, I had seen magpies kill a little one. I kept an eye on the courtyard to make sure it wouldn't happen again. I began to worry that the chick had fallen out of its nest and since it couldn't fly yet, it was stranded on the ground to die. The day before, I had seen a dead female thrush on a neighbor's roof and thought it might have been its mother. Then, a bit later, the chick wasn't there anymore. I looked around the yard and found it collapsed near a bush. I was afraid it was near death and automatically placed my hand over it to give him energy. Soon, I heard chirping, and then it stood back up. I thought the best I could do was nudge it under the bush. At least it would be protected from magpies.

About an hour later, I went outside to join my husband, who was barbecuing. I heard a chirping and to my surprise and delight, the baby bird and his father were perched on a very low branch.

The following morning, my husband noticed the male thrush followed by not only the roly-poly baby, but also by a second, skinny one. We realized then that the mother had probably been killed, and the father was left to take care of both chicks.

My story with the birds didn't end there. After this incident, when I would sit on the couch near the courtyard-side window, the father bird would often land on the windowsill and stand there looking at me through the glass. One time, the door to the courtyard was open, and he flew inside the house. As for the baby birds, we saw them come back to play in the courtyard throughout the winter. We knew it was them because they were very recognizable—they kept their earlier appearance. One was "roly-poly" and the other one slender. On snowy days, they sometimes came to the door opening into the courtyard. I could see their little footprints all the way to the top of the stairs.

It was obvious there was a very special connection and recognition from the birds. The little visits they made were Winks from Above that made me smile. To remain connected with the Spirits of Nature, whether covered with feathers, hair, bark, or petals, brings so much pleasure.

CHAPTER 11

I Am Not Alone

Occasionally, I experience one of those little moments in life that remind me that I'm not alone. Here is a collection of moments that, while small, I have not taken for granted.

The Shamans in the Rain

To celebrate the birthday of a shaman friend of mine, a group of fellow shamans organized a big outdoor celebration, with a bonfire planned for later that evening. It was at the end of March when the weather in Brussels can still be quite chilly. Sure enough, it rained all day the day of the event, and it was still drizzling when we arrived in the late afternoon.

We all assumed we wouldn't be able to stay very long, since most of the activities were to be outdoors and would have to be cancelled. We went ahead with the first activity, during which a group of us were going to play drums. The minute we started to play, a pale ray of sun appeared in the sky. We were all so much in awe that we literally missed a beat and stopped drumming for a minute or so. It was stunning. After a chilly, grey, and rainy day, how could that be?

Although it was already late in the day, the light was so beautiful and such a joyful gift from Above—a Wink to let us know that our Animal Spirits, our Spirit Guides, and the Spirits of Nature were also going to partake in our activities and rejoice with us. All the outside activities were held as planned, and the gathering lasted late into evening.

So many Synchronicities happened to me that day that it would take too long to describe all of them. However, the most significant one is the confirmation I received from several shamans I had never previously met that my recently deceased mother was watching over me.

The Cash Register

I've found that solitary, long walks in the mountain snow are always conducive to reflection. It's very hard to have negative thoughts when Nature is covered with a brilliant veil of pristine snow. All is silent except for the steps I take with my snowshoes, the trickling sounds of water running in tiny creeks, a bird leaving its perch when I approach, the thump of snow falling from a branch, and my breath as I climb a steep path. On the way back I love to stop in the village to get a raspberry cream cake with hot cocoa.

One day, I had just come back from a 10k walk through the snow and ice in the stunning Bavarian mountains. It was sunny and very beautiful. I stopped at a store but was in a hurry because I was supposed to meet my husband at our hotel, and I was running late. As soon as I reached the long line of people waiting to go through the only available cash register, a store employee walked toward me and pointed for me to go to the other, unmanned cash register. I felt a bit embarrassed because I thought someone in front of me should have been invited to start the new line. I also thought it was strange because normally, a cashier would have simply opened the new cash register and people would have shifted lanes to line up.

As I paid, other people started to line up behind me but then, for some reason, the saleswoman closed her cash register and left. It really puzzled me because the other line was still at least as long as before.

This was a Wink from Above. Thank you up there! It was one of those times when I wonder if I've stepped into another dimension.

A Laugh from Above

It's not unusual for me to get up very early in the morning and sit in a lounge chair in the bedroom to meditate, write, and sometimes connect with my Guides. One day, my husband got up to make coffee and, not realizing I was "astral travelling," touched my leg gently to ask if I wanted him to bring me some coffee. Being awakened so suddenly from a trance-like channeling with my Guides freaked me out, and I screamed and cried for a minute or so.

When I came back to my senses, I heard snickering. One of my Guides made a comment that, at the time, seemed kind of judgmental; "T'was a bit dramatic, wasn't it?"

I was a bit put off, but it didn't last long. To be judgmental is a human trait. Our Guides don't have it. I took it as someone mocking me and didn't like it at the time because I was too shaken to see the humor in it. But eventually, I realized that it was very funny. The voice was so clear that I still hear it once in a while. And today, when I think of that episode, it makes me smile. Yes, our Guides have a great sense of humor.

The Uber Ride

A few years ago, at the end of my stay in Paris, I called an Uber to pick me up and take me from the city to a hotel near the Charles de Gaulle Airport. My plane back to the States was leaving early the following morning, and I always find it less stressful to spend the night before at a hotel near the airport.

The driver was a young man. He was very polite, but we barely had left the hotel before I started feeling tension. I could tell something was bothering him. We started talking, and soon he began to share all the anger he had toward his ex-girlfriend. He was expressing quite vehemently how much he wanted to hurt her. I let him vent for a while but finally had to say, "You have to be very careful; you'll hurt yourself a lot in the process." I don't remember exactly how he responded.

This ride usually takes at least one hour, but the next thing I heard was a voice saying, "we've arrived." I had fallen asleep and woke up already in front of my hotel near the airport. This was a surprise, but even more surprising was the fact that the young man had tears in his eyes. He thanked me for my advice and told me I was right. Puzzled, I got out of the car, and he helped me with my luggage. Then he asked if he could get a hug. It was a surprising request because it's usually not something a young man in his position would ask a woman, but, of course, I hugged him. He thanked me again and said he would follow my advice. But I didn't know what the advice was. I had fallen asleep and didn't remember saying anything. That was odd.

Seeing how the young man was so affected by what I don't remember saying, I knew I must have entered a state of spontaneous Channeling. Could I have found the right words to help him calm down if I had remained in a normal state? Maybe not. It must have been an intervention from Above. After all, the driver was extremely angry, and that's never a safe state to be in when driving for over an hour on a very busy highway. Maybe it was an intervention by our Guardian Angels and Guides.

The Overheard Conversation

When my friend Naomi was in her twenties and living on the West Coast, she had dental surgery. Her parents were driving her home, and she was in the back seat of the car, still somewhat drugged from the procedure. Suddenly and clearly, she heard a conversation between her younger brother and his wife. Which was odd as they lived 3000 miles away on the East Coast, and there were no cell phones at that time. Naomi heard someone say "Darn! The condom broke and we're pregnant." They already had two children, a boy and a girl, and Naomi was aware that they hadn't anticipated having any more. She listened in amazement, thinking it was strange and assuming it must be the effect of the drugs.

A couple of weeks later, her brother called their mother to announce that his wife was pregnant with their third, unplanned child. Naomi decided to not say anything about the conversation she had "heard" in the car because it was just too weird to bring up. Years later, during a conversation with her brother about his youngest child, he explained that "He really wanted to come into this world because we had an accident—the condom broke."

So, it wasn't the drugs after all! Naomi was amazed that what she had "heard" was validated—she experienced a moment of Clairaudience. Nonetheless, she was glad she hadn't shared the experience with anyone. It could have made her brother and his wife quite uncomfortable.

The Book by the Gate

One Saturday night, as my husband and I were leaving for the Miss Brazil-Belgium competition, I noticed a book titled *Ce Soir, Je Veillerai Sur Toi (Tonight, I'll Watch Over You)* sitting on the electrical box just outside our entry gate. We had seen junk items and empty cans left on that spot for years, but never a book. As we were in a hurry, I grabbed it and put it inside the courtyard on the patio without even looking at what it was all about.

When we came back, I discovered the book told the story of an Angel helping a little girl. This happened at the beginning of my training as a healer, after I had spent the week getting acquainted with the Ascended Masters, our team of Celestial Helpers and the Angels. I found that "gift" quite unusual but very appropriate.

CHAPTER 12

Assistance/Help

As help comes from many different sources, it's important to not discount any of the Signs. Even if they seem odd at the time, they are often a reminder just when it's needed. They might provide an answer we need right away, guide us in the right direction, or confirm that we are at the right place.

The Spider Webs

Early in the morning, I love to do a dance improvisation/meditation—outside in Nature when possible. A few years ago, I was attending a couple of week-long seminars at the Monroe Institute, located in the beautiful Blue Ridge Mountains, and part of their morning routine included an optional yoga class before breakfast. I went once but decided I would prefer to start my day in communion with the gorgeous Nature surrounding us. So, the next morning, I walked to my favorite spot in a field beside a magnificent, six-foot-tall pink quartz rock from Brazil, that had been a gift to the Institute. The open field was surrounded by mountains, still dark against a sky barely lit by the rising sun.

I could see many white spots in the grass, especially in the area where I wanted to dance. At first, I thought they were flowers. But looking closer, I saw that they actually were tiny spider webs—a type I had never seen before. As the sun rose higher in the sky, the dew adorned each web with tiny crystal beads. What a beautiful sight! I felt like a little child stepping into a magical world and started dancing surrounded by all my new friends.

As the days went on, I continued to dance among the dew-covered webs and also noticed other interesting webs. Unlike the small ones, these covered large portions of many bushes. I really didn't understand why I felt so attracted by their design. I don't mind spiders—I even talked to them when I was a child. But that had been a very long time ago.

Three weeks later, I had to go back to France to visit my dad. He had recently been diagnosed with colon cancer and had to have surgery to remove part of his intestines. I found it odd that a surgical mesh hadn't been placed internally before closing him back up. As a result, his severed muscles couldn't hold him very well and his insides were protruding under the dressing. He was of course in great discomfort and, as an energy healer, I decided to work on him.

As I was preparing to start, all of a sudden, I realized why spiders had recently come into my life. I had to create an energy web to help contain his intestines and alleviate the pain while he was recovering. Each day, I worked on tightening this virtual web until my father was able to wear a special girdle. It didn't heal or replace what was missing, of course, but at least I was able to lessen the discomfort he was experiencing and probably help him heal faster.

This story is a reminder that we need to be very alert to any Signs—even those, like the spider webs, that seem strange. It's also a reminder to always stay in contact with our inner child and follow its guidance. I'm full of gratitude for the help and inspiration Nature provided me with on that day. I now have another tool in my healer's bag.

Spotify Music

I had begun to attend a very special class called "The Sacred Container" with Christine Kloser, and our first week's assignment was to work on our spiritual alignment. I made a pledge to myself to resume my dance/meditation practice the following day. I hadn't been in a very good place and needed to snap out of it. My dance meditation has always been a good way for me to clear my mind.

The next morning, I went on our terrace and selected Spotify on my iPad. I chose a channel called "Stress Relief" and started a slow warm-up dance. The music was beautiful, and I didn't remember hearing it before. So, I went to check what it was called and to my great surprise and delight, the title of the piece was *Spiritual Alignment!* I felt giddy and ready to dance a happy dance.

I had been frustrated because for the previous two months, I had been feeling totally out of touch with my Guardians, and I hadn't received any Signs from them. Until that morning. Out of thousands of musical choices, what were the odds that the piece that played first would address the very thing I was supposed to be working on? By doing what I promised myself I would do, the connection was re-established.

The next day, I went outside to dance and tuned into Spotify's Stress Relief channel on my iPad. The first music that played was again *Spiritual Alignment* and to my surprise, it played again and again and again. The third time it re-started, I went to check what was going on and noticed it was on a loop. I didn't remember selecting that option. I didn't even know I had it.

This was amazing, and it indeed validated what I intended to write in my book. I'm so grateful to have been invited to join this very special course. From day one, the results have been beyond my expectations.

I took this as a validation and encouragement of what I'm doing. Another one of those Winks from Above.

The Technician

One morning, two technicians came to check the connections on our home theater system.

Brad (the assistant tech, who was probably close to retirement) and I had a very unusual conversation. When he found out we had lived in Brussels, he told me how he wanted to visit the battlefields of Europe. Then he went on to describe his father fighting in Iwo Jima, and a painting he'd started after the description of a battle by his father that he was having difficulty finishing. I felt it was right to ask him if he was "in contact" with his father. "Oh yes," he said, "his spirit is even present in our house."

He recounted various strange events that happened to some members of his family, including one of them cancelling a flight at the last minute and the plane subsequently crashing, which was similar to my own experience. The most recent happened around Bastille Day 2016, when a nephew who lived in France was supposed to go to a celebration in Nice and watch the fireworks from la Promenade des Anglais. He was delayed when the friends he was going with could not leave as early as they originally intended. Later, in precisely the location where they planned to watch the display, a truck driver deliberately drove into the crowd, killing 86 people and wounding 458. That delay might have saved their lives.

This encounter happened at a crucial moment, when I was questioning the validity of the topic of this book. It was especially strange because Brad barely showed any interest in the technical problems we were experiencing. He only wanted to talk with me about the Synchronicities he and his family were experiencing, while his colleague performed all the tests and spoke with my husband. It was as though he was there to let me know I was on the right track.

I take it as a Wink from Above. Thank you so much, Guides, for watching over me!

Mont Saint Michel and the Tibetan Monks

I had been planning to attend the "Laude," which is the 7:00 a.m. church service at the Abbey of Mont Saint Michel in France. However, my husband and I both woke up too late. It wasn't until later that morning that we finally reached the top of the Mont and went inside to visit the beautiful church.

Just behind the altar was a visitor's book in which we could write a few notes about our visit to Saint Michel. As I was signing it, I noticed a priest placing barricades to prevent visitors from entering the area we had just come from. I don't know why, but I felt I needed to ask him to bless my pendulum, which I always carried with me as part of my healing kit.

"Father, would it be a sacrilege to ask you to bless this?"

"Yes, because it is considered magic."

"Father, I use this tool to help others."

"You can only help others through the love of Jesus."

Why argue? So, I apologized and retraced my steps to exit on the opposite side of the altar. My husband was there waiting for me and with a nod of his head indicated a group of Tibetan Buddhists meditating reverently in front of the Virgin Mary. I joined them and sat on the floor to meditate too; tears started to run down my face. It's funny, of all the colors I could wear, that morning, I had decided to wear a jacket the same dark red as their robes.

I realized the Holy Good Thursday mass was going to be celebrated and told my husband I wanted to stay and attend it. We sat with the Buddhist group—some of them were kneeling on the floor and bowing all the way to the ground like they do at the pagoda. I noticed that near the altar, some of the Catholic nuns were also kneeling on the floor and bowing all the way to the ground. Interesting. At one point, one of the lamas, who was four to five rows in front of us, turned back and looked at me. Our eyes locked for a few seconds. It didn't feel awkward, just very peaceful.

The nuns sang through the service and at times it transported me to another place. When I closed my eyes, I could see a gray mass surrounded by a white light. That bright light was in the shape of a person holding or wrapped around something gray. The gray fluctuated from medium to light with some very pale spots here and there. Nothing scary, it felt very peaceful. Several times during the service, tears ran down my face. A little child, a couple of rows in front of me, turned around to briefly look at me. He had a sweet expression with a very faint smile that moved me.

What was happening? This occurred at the beginning of my training as a healer—a time during which I experienced many Synchronicities and Winks. I believe it was a Sign showing me I was on the right path.

A Question for My Guides

One night before falling asleep, I asked for guidance from the Above. I placed a notebook and pen right beside me, although since I was very new at using this technique, I didn't know whether it would work or not. When I awoke as usual around 3:30 a.m., I thought, "All right, I'm ready to listen." I sat there in the dark, pen in hand, hand on my notebook, and waited...and waited. Nothing. A bit frustrated, I put my notebook and pen away, rolled on my side and was ready to go back to sleep.

Suddenly, in my mind's eye, a crowd appeared, marching toward me. I could hear the brouhaha of chanting and saw that some people in the crowd seemed to be carrying banners, but they were too far away for me to be able to read what was written on them. It looked like a large, peaceful demonstration. As they came closer and passed right below me, I was able to hear their chant: "We want you to write your book. Stop procrastinating." To emphasize their message, those same words were also written on the banners. The crowd was so large that I couldn't see the end of it. Then, *poof*, they were all gone.

They were absolutely right about my procrastinating. They came when I needed to be reminded that the time to start my book was NOW. This experience of Clairvoyance and Clairaudience was the start of many nightly contacts I had with my Guides.

My Dad's Wife's Camera

During one of my dad's visits to Brussels, we left his wife in one of the Belgian specialty stores and went to visit Saint Nicolas, a very old and beautiful church dating back to the 13th century. My dad decided to light a candle and pray in front of the statue of Saint Antony. He put his camera down on a chair and knelt on the pew in front of him.

We then returned to the store where we had left his wife. She looked at my dad's hands and asked, "Where is my camera?"

My dad replied, "Oh sh...!" He turned around and dashed toward the door. I ran after him. "I probably left it on the chair when I knelt down," he said. A few minutes later, we were back at the church walking very fast toward the statue of Saint Antony. There was some irony there—he is the patron saint of lost things.

We both looked very carefully. There was nothing on the chair he thought he left it on or on the chairs nearby. There was also nothing underneath. Very disappointed, we headed for the exit. However, just as we were almost at the door, I felt the need to turn to my left and walk again down the aisle leading to the statue of Saint Antony. I don't know why. It wasn't a conscious decision.

I could see a dark shadow under one of the chairs. As I came closer, I couldn't believe it. There was the camera.

What caused me to turn back toward the statue of Saint Anthony? Was it a moment of Claircognizance, or one of my Guides leading me back to that spot?

I can't explain, except my feet took me to the left instead of straight out of the door. It's like I was guided to go back where I had already been to discover that there was something under the chair. We both had looked very carefully before but there was nothing, so we were stunned.

What I learned from this is that I'm not alone. None of us are. We have Guides watching over us and if we reach out to them via prayers, meditation, or even just a strong wish, we might get an answer or some form of help.

CHAPTER 13

Synchronicity

Sometimes in life, we experience a succession of incredible events that put us at the exact right place at the exact right time. These Synchronicities have occurred throughout my life and began even before I came to earth.

Without Hiroshima, I would never have been born. During World War II, after the Allies landed in Normandy in 1944 and liberated France, the country was able to recreate an army called the First Army. When volunteers were asked to join, my father, still a teenager, took it as the opportunity to get out of his miserable life. In February 1945, he was placed in the newly created "Infanterie Coloniale." He was sent from Versailles to Germany for training, and then another opportunity arose—to go fight in Japan under the U.S. flag with the promise of being able to emigrate to the United States afterwards.

My father had signed up—but the Hiroshima bombing changed everything. After it occurred, all the French volunteers preparing for Japan were sent instead to Indochina, which then was still a French colony. That's how my father ended up in Vietnam, where he met my mother and where I was born in 1949.

In 1995, 50 years after the Hiroshima tragedy, my husband's new assignment took us from Italy to Japan. I knew I had to visit that city because of the special meaning it had for me. To arrive for the 50th anniversary was a Sign I should not miss the occasion, especially since I would never have been born had the horrific event not happened. I had the opportunity to take our then nine-year-old son and teach him about the atrocities caused by a nuclear bomb. I prepared him by reading him the story of Sadako Sasaki, the girl who died of the after-effects of the bomb, and the legend of the Hiroshima Peace Cranes. She wanted to make 1000 origami paper cranes before she died, and when she wasn't able to complete her wish, her classmates did it for her.

We made a large necklace of paper cranes so my son could give it as an offering for peace beside Sadako's statue. We also rang the Peace Bell to call for peace in the world. The visit left quite an impression on my young boy. For me, the most emotional moment happened in the Peace Museum. In front of a watch found after the explosion, which had stopped at the precise moment of impact, an old woman was talking to a couple of young children. Perhaps they were her grandchildren or great-grandchildren. I could not understand what she was telling them, but I could feel her deep sorrow.

It was amazing to me to realize how two events that seem totally unrelated can be indissociable. I wouldn't have been born if Hiroshima hadn't happened. And what were the odds that I would move to Japan and be able to visit the city on the 50th anniversary of this tragedy?

Events and periods like this make me realize that I am—we all are—much more than our physical bodies.

Mount Fuji

Climbing Mount Fuji was on my bucket list, but at the time we moved to Japan it was not possible. It was already off-season. The climbing trail was open only for a couple months in the summer and only when the weather allowed. I was disappointed that we'd have to wait until the following summer. But somehow, I got lucky. The Secretary of the U.S. Air Force came to Japan for an official visit, and since she and her husband were avid climbers, she told her Japanese hosts that they wanted to hike Mount Fuji. Suddenly, the mountain was deemed safe enough to be reopened, but only for the Secretary and the people accompanying her. The senior military officers from our Air Force base were invited to join her party, and their spouses could go too. With my husband being in the band of volunteers, of course I jumped at the opportunity! Our party of about 20 were the only people on the mountain except Japanese personnel manning each of the stamp stations. They were reopened specifically so we could have our wooden walking sticks branded with the logo showing the altitudes all the way up to 12,600 feet.

This is a perfect example of Synchronicity—I had a very strong desire to climb this sacred mountain and didn't want to wait until the next summer. In fact, the following year, my husband didn't have the time to go, but thankfully, I was able to do a night ascension with our then 10-year-old son. We arrived at the summit to enjoy the magic of the rising of the sun, which was an unforgettable mystical experience.

Point to Ponder

Have you ever had a strong wish that seemed impossible to fulfill but came true despite the odds?

The Old Man in Chicago

When we lived in Washington, D.C., I worked as a consultant at the Academy of Fashion and Image. Helping people to "find their colors" was part of the program. However, I gradually began to feel it wasn't right to teach something I found superficial. The world was changing, and my level of consciousness was rising. I was still using the combinations of colors and textures the program advocated for myself, but I stopped teaching it to others and gradually started to wear mostly black.

After a while, except for a few colors here and there, black was the only choice I had in my wardrobe. But one day years later, I had the urge to wear colors and have fun experimenting with them. This urge coincided with my trip to Charlottesville, Virginia, to hunt for a house to buy. During my five weeks there, I had so much fun wearing a variety of colors again. I added more pieces to my wardrobe and wore lots of combinations, and many people stopped me in the street to tell me how much they loved my outfits.

After a few days of receiving compliments, an idea popped up. *Could I use colors in my healing practice?*

I was in Chicago's O'Hare Airport, waiting in line to board my plane to return to Brussels when a man in front of me complimented me on what I was wearing. He talked at length, in a way I would have considered a come-on had it been from someone else, but this was different. He was a slender, tall, and elegant older man, dressed in a white linen suit and a pale-colored hat—similar to the mysterious man I met in the train in France. I didn't feel uncomfortable even though he was showering me with compliments. Instead, it gave me the incentive to do more research regarding healing with colors. I thought it would be neat to have as another tool to use in Energy Healing.

The day after I returned to Brussels, I was reading the local newspaper for expatriates when I came across an ad about an upcoming course called Healing with Colors, taught by Marcia O'Regan. I was initially thrilled but soon disappointed when I realized it was offered precisely at a time I was going to be in Lisbon, Portugal, for a healing seminar. I decided to call the woman to find out when she would offer the course again, and she said that since it was the first time she was teaching it in Brussels, she didn't know. However, she was willing to change the dates to accommodate my schedule. Wow! I couldn't believe how lucky I was.

I believe the man at the airport was the same Guide who I met in France. Amazingly, many of the strangers who appeared throughout my life when I needed help were tall, slender old men, impeccably dressed in black or in white. Thanks to my Guide, I was able to not only attend all of Marcia's fantastic "Glow Your True Colours" classes on color analysis but to also take the next step to get a certificate in Chromotherapy and add a new tool to my healer's bag. Talk about Synchronicities.

Our Boy and His Dog

From the year he was two until the year our son turned 13, we moved almost every two years, to places all around the world. This was not easy for him. We always moved at the beginning of summer when school was out, and as our child wasn't very outgoing, it was challenging for him to make friends right away.

When he was seven, we had just arrived in Italy from Germany, and I decided to take him camping for a few weeks at a large, beachfront campground on the Adriatic shore. My husband couldn't join us due to work, so my son and I shared our very comfortable caravan that we parked right by the beach.

On day one, a cute little tri-color dachshund showed up to play with our son. The dog had apparently been abandoned. He came and went throughout the day, but each night, we found him lying on top of our son's camp bed under the awning attached to the caravan. At first, I was a bit concerned that it wasn't very healthy to let a stray dog sleep with our son. But when I saw the joy he brought to our little boy, my concerns faded away. After all, he looked very healthy, well-fed, and he was such a loving little dog.

Our son really wanted to be able to adopt him, and he begged his dad to allow it. After many back-and-forth phone conversations, he received the green light. The next morning, I sat him and the little dog on my bed to inform them of the decision. Suddenly, the dog started "talking" in long, modulated sounds that resembled more the mooing of a cow than any bark or whine that might come from a dog. It was a strange sound we never had heard before or afterwards. It was as though he was telling us his life story; it lasted for at least 10 minutes. To this day, we still can't understand how this happened and why. The only thing I know is that our boy had a wonderful little friend that came into his life to ease his loneliness and who became his constant, faithful companion for the next 13 years.

I thanked our son's Guide and Guardian Angel for sending him exactly what he needed, a fun and loving little friend. They became inseparable.

Retirement Planning

About three years before my husband was due to retire, we started to think about where we would like to go. We lived in Brussels. My husband is American, I'm French, and we had lived in many countries around the world. This didn't make the decision very easy. We had a very beautiful home in the center of Brussels, but we needed to go someplace where there was more sun. We had lived in and loved several Asian and European countries but still couldn't make up our minds. Portugal was a brief contender, and France was of course very high on the list, so we started looking at the pros and the cons of retiring there. The pros were numerous, but too many cons made us hesitate.

That's when we turned towards the U.S. Although we visited my husband's family in the States a couple of times a year, we hadn't lived there for 26 years. My husband thought it might be time to give it some serious consideration.

So, in which part of the States would we want to live? During an OBE, I found myself above a forested mountainous area and I thought that it was maybe in California. I searched the map with my pendulum, but it always indicated the central part of the East Coast. We started to search via the Internet and the city of Charlottesville, Virginia kept popping up. When we discovered that the city was located near the Blue Ridge mountains and in the central part of the East Coast, matching what I had seen, we started to become interested in learning more. We had lived in Washington, D.C., and spent a lot of time in Virginia Beach and Norfolk but had never visited that university and historical town.

My husband suggested we fly there the following month and spend a few days visiting the area. Since it would be February, it would be an ideal time to see if we would like the town and the area during the worst of the winter weather. It had snowed the week before, but it was beautiful when we arrived. We fell in love with the town. It was everything we were hoping for and even more.

Of course, there's also a little more Winking from Above in this story. About five years before, when spending time in Bavaria, I went to the military base library to check out a book. I chose one of the "Miss Murphy" books by Rita Mae Brown, a charming series about the adventures of a woman who lives in Crozet, Virginia, with her clever cat. I loved so much the description of the beautiful area, the delightful people, and the adventures that I read 15 or so of the books in the collection. I often thought how wonderful it would be to live in such a place.

It turns out that Crozet isn't a fictitious place. Located near the city of Charlottesville, it's a village that's growing into a small town. Amazingly, our son and daughter-in-law eventually bought a townhome in Crozet, and that's where they now live with our granddaughters.

To have picked up a Miss Murphy book at random, in Germany, many years before we decided to move to Charlottesville is quite extraordinary—especially because it introduced me to the people, the scenery, and the general lifestyle that we now have. I loved all the descriptions in the book, and it helped me move into our new life with great ease. It was all so familiar.

What were the odds?

Also near Charlottesville is The Monroe Institute, a place I heard of and read about even before thinking of moving to the States. I was hoping to be able to visit it someday, but its location didn't resonate with me at the time because, while I dreamed of attending some of the classes, I never thought I'd be able to do so (this was before they started offering classes online). But there it was, just 40 minutes south of Charlottesville. Needless to say, since we moved here, I have attended eight wonderful seminars in the beautiful Blue Ridge Mountains location.

Still uncertain about moving, we came back in August just to check how comfortable it was in the heat of summer. The humid, hot weather didn't bother us, and we still loved the area and the way of living so much that we hired a realtor to start searching for a home.

Back in Brussels, we kept in contact via the Internet and found a home we thought would be perfect for us. The pictures and the videos our realtor sent convinced us it was our ideal home. So, we decided to buy it and made an offer. Very excited, we signed everything electronically then went to bed.

Around 4:30 a.m. I found myself wide awake. I went to check my email. My heart missed a beat. Someone else had made an offer on the house at the same time as we had, and the sellers chose the other buyers. We had planned to fly to Charlottesville the following week! The realtor explained that "we lost out due to circumstances beyond our control…distance."

I was crushed. I couldn't breathe. I really wanted to share the bad news, but it was too early to wake my husband up.

A bit later, I went back to my computer. On my screen was a picture of a house under a dark, starry sky with the message "Once you make a decision, the Universe conspires to Make It Happen." Was that a Wink from Above telling me that all would be well, and I just had to believe?

We went to Charlottesville the following week as planned. We visited the house that we had made the offer on, "just in case the transaction doesn't go through," as the realtor put it. I was heartbroken.

After we left, we passed a house further up the same street. The realtor mentioned that it would be going on the market in three days. Would we like to visit it? She called the realtor who was handling the listing and we were able to visit right away.

As soon as we entered, we felt at home. The main floor overlooked a beautiful wooded area and a little creek. It felt like being in a tree house. The owner, a professor of astronomy at The University of Virginia who happened to be of Indian descent, was there. He explained that the terrace was built to face the east so he could meditate to the rising sun. "And so do we," we told him.

He went on to explain that in a specific corner of the foundation of the house, an offering package dedicated to Ganesh was buried according to the rites of Jainism. We exclaimed that we also loved Ganesh and had a large, antic bronze statue from Nepal that would feel right at home in that house. It was amazing to realize that this house had become available at just the right time. It was the perfect home for us, down to the protection embedded in the foundation.

We bought it right away.

Had our earlier offer been accepted the week before, we would never have known about the house that is now our beloved and cherished home.

We can see the house we almost bought from our home. Another house has since been built very close to it, and we wouldn't have liked that at all. More recently, the lovely view from the back of the house that attracted us in the first place changed. Across the small river, part of the wood was cut to build a few commercial buildings, which has completely changed the vista from the house.

We now understand that the deal fell apart because a larger and better house for us was coming on the market a few days later. We're very thankful to have been guided away from the house we thought we wanted. Yes, "Once you make a decision, the Universe conspires to Make It Happen".

Point to Ponder

Have you ever had to face the disappointment of not getting what you were dreaming of, like a job, a promotion, or a relationship, only to discover a better opportunity soon afterward? Or have you later found out details that would have made you regret ever achieving that dream?

The Phone Number

In 2013, my dear friend Naomi was an administrator in the advancement department of an eastern university. One day, a new receptionist left a scrap of paper on her desk with a phone number, not realizing it was intended for someone else.

When Naomi picked up the paper and looked at the strange number, she felt a strong energy. Something told her she needed to return the call. So, she dialed the number. This one decision set off a series of Synchronicities that changed many lives.

The person Naomi reached wanted to make a large gift to the university in honor of an administrator who, 40 years earlier, had helped him get financial support to go to the college. Amazingly, Naomi knew and had just visited with the elderly, since-retired administrator the night before. She was the perfect person to talk with the donor, connect him back to the administrator, and arrange for the gift for the university.

Still feeling a great deal of energy and not understanding why, Naomi flew to meet the donor, listened to his story, and talked about the administrator who had been so kind to him years ago. The donor then doubled his very generous gift, benefiting the university and providing Naomi with accolades at her job.

On the way home, Naomi stopped off in New Jersey to see her daughter, son-in-law, and new grandchild. The couple's dream was to move near Naomi and their families in the D.C. area, some four hours away. They disliked the urban area where they lived and told her their jobs were "soul-killing"—they had been looking for new positions for three years to no avail due to the recession. However, when Naomi walked in, she spotted a contract on their dining table they were to sign *that very day* to buy a house in the same area. They had given up on their dream!

Naomi took her daughter and granddaughter to lunch at a restaurant in a nearby town, when suddenly, her daughter heard her husband's voice. She was quite surprised to find him in a town away from his job. He explained that he had received a phone call, out of the blue, to meet an old colleague from out of town. The colleague's purpose was to tell him to apply for a particular job in a town close to where their families lived.

What were the odds? A month later, the ecstatic young couple and their baby moved to a town near their families, started jobs they loved, bought a house, and settled in.

Publishing a Book

As I explained at the beginning of this book, the idea to write about the Synchronicities in my life came to me during my month-long stay at the hospital in Brussels. I had just gone through an extraordinary sequence of events that led from a dire situation to a very positive outcome. I wanted to share the importance of being aware of the Signs placed on our path to guide us when we need help.

In February 2020, after coming back from my post-surgery check-up in Europe, I had a burning desire to continue my writing project. With the number of cases of Covid-19 increasing rapidly, I started to stay home more than usual. It was a perfect time to seriously think about the next phase. Having more time meant it was the perfect time to start writing a transformational book.

Writing a book is not easy, but it is also very challenging to have it published. That's when I received an email from a friend informing me *her* book had just been published, encouraging me to check out the publishing company she worked with. I did, but I was unimpressed. Then, the following day I got an email from Kris Kyle with information about Christine Kloser, an award-winning publisher and transformational author coach, who happened to be holding a free, five-day webinar beginning in just a few days. I registered and absolutely loved each presentation. On the fifth day, without hesitation, I signed up with Christine Kloser's program.

I realized I needed a new laptop to start writing my book. My small MacBook Air had been fantastic to travel with, but it was getting old, and I would be more comfortable spending hours writing with a larger screen.

I thought a MacPro 13-inch would be ideal. Not too big, not too small and light enough to carry around. My husband and I went to our local Best Buy. But as this was at the beginning of the Covid-19 pandemic, the atmosphere was very different. A limited number of customers were allowed in the store at a time, and everyone wore masks. Once we got inside, most of the laptops had been sold and they were no Mac computers of any size left. We asked if we could place an order, but we were told we would have to make an appointment with the Apple manager, who…just happened to walk by at that moment. She confirmed that everything had been sold and made a sweeping gesture to show us all the shelves were empty, even the caged area way up on top.

That's when I noticed there was one lonely box on the very top shelf of that caged area.

I pointed it out to her. Very surprised, she climbed up the ladder to check it out. Yes, there was one Mac left, and it was exactly the model I wanted.

When you follow your intuition, events just seem to happen. I had to contain myself—my inner child wanted to jump and squeal with joy, but I only smiled and thanked my Guides quietly.

I have a feeling the Archangel Gabriel orchestrated this amazing series of events that led me to the right author's coach at the right time. He is usually who I connect with when it comes to writing, along with my Guide.

Point to Ponder

Having read about the real-life Synchronicities that happened throughout my life, can you remember any times when a succession of events led you to a very desirable situation, with almost no effort on your part?

CHAPTER 14

Dreams

When you sleep, all your beliefs retreat and don't filter what your Spirit Guides are sharing with you. Because of this, it's very useful to set your intention before going to sleep. You can often solve some of your thorniest problems and get answers to your deepest questions when your conscious mind is out of the way.

The Lost Cat

While we were living in Brussels, our cat, Shadow, was free to roam our property at night. Our garden was big enough for her to explore and even if she went on the roof of the garage, the walls and the gate were too tall for her to escape into the street.

One night during a storm, we had a very strong wind—so strong a chimney fell off the roof of a building across from our courtyard. It damaged the glass roof of a nearby covered courtyard, but only some debris fell into our garden.

A couple of days later, I couldn't find Shadow and started asking neighbors if they had seen her. Nobody had. Then, three days after she went missing, I had a dream. I saw Shadow in a dark cellar with a very peculiar feature. There was a fireplace. A fireplace in a cellar? I had never heard of that.

The next day, in the afternoon, I decided to go to our little grocery store around the corner. As I entered, I heard a woman complaining to the store owner that he needed to do something about a noise coming from behind the door of his new, unopened store down the street. The owner said that he didn't have the time and walked away. The woman moved to the front of the store and was going to leave. That's when I felt compelled to do something I would never do. I ran after her and asked her what she was discussing with the store owner.

She said that for three days, she had heard a cat behind the door of the store down the street, and since the renovations had stopped and the building was empty, she was afraid the cat was trapped. I asked her to take me there. As soon as we arrived, I heard a cat. There was enough space for me to put my hand under the door. I felt a little head against the palm of my hand and knew it was Shadow.

I went back to the store to ask the owner to please open the door because it was my cat that was trapped. He didn't have the key but kindly called his nephew to bring one. About an hour later, we opened the door, but Shadow was frightened when she saw the young man. She ran to the back of the store and down a stairwell leading to the cellar. Because of the renovations, the electricity had been turned off and it was very dark. The young man turned on his cell phone and we followed the dim light into the cellar to find the cat.

There was a fireplace in the cellar, just like I had seen in my dream. I was so surprised it made me shiver. I wrapped my cat inside my jacket and went back home, puzzled by what I had just experienced.

Clearly that dream was an instance of Clairvoyance. Still, there was more to it than that. What were the odds that I would go to the store at the precise moment a lady was talking to the manager about my cat? Did my cat communicate with me via a dream to let me know where she was? I accepted it as wonderful help provided by the Above. I'm glad I was awake enough to be able to receive it.

Point to Ponder

Have you ever dreamed of an event that occurred soon after?

The Missing Credit Card Machine

One day, when I was working for the Academy of Fashion and Image in Virginia, the credit card machine was nowhere to be found. We looked everywhere and wondered what could have happened to it, but never figured out where it was.

After a few nights, I had a dream. I saw the credit card machine in a storage room, way up on the top shelf, to the right. So, the next day, when I went to the office, the first thing I did was to go to that room to check. The top shelf was too high for me to see what was on it, so I had to pull up a small ladder.

There it was, exactly where I had seen it in my dream.

How did that happen? Was that simply Clairvoyance, or did I have an OBE while dreaming?

Point to Ponder

Have you ever had a dream that showed you where an item you were searching for was hidden?

Learning How to Say No

While living in Virginia, I signed up for a week-long healing seminar in France. A friend was also going to attend, and I thought it would be fun to attend together. However, in the meantime, I experienced an unfortunate situation with the teacher and consequently didn't feel like spending time in her presence. However, I didn't know how to get out of the promise I had made to join the course. For weeks, this uncomfortable thought was in and out of my mind. As the dreaded date approached, my anxiety was growing.

Shortly before my scheduled departure for France, I was taking a seminar at the Monroe Institute. One of our exercises was to set an intention very clearly and follow a guided meditation. Unfortunately, I was so focused on my upcoming situation that I felt very unsettled. I fell asleep and wasn't able to hear the important Message from Above that could help me get out of the seminar.

The instructor told me that it didn't matter. I had still *received* the Message even though I didn't remember *hearing* it.

That night, I went to bed quite perturbed to be missing the answer I was seeking. During the night, in my dreams, there were constant battles between the idea of going and the idea of not going. It was horrible. I tossed and turned and slept fitfully, waking in the middle of the night, feeling I had to honor my promise. I was so upset. I knew I couldn't possibly get a lot out of the course when I was experiencing so much antagonism against the teacher in France.

Fortunately, I was able to go back to sleep. When I woke up in the morning, I felt a bit tired but totally at peace. I had received the perfect excuse to get out of the situation.

I don't remember dreaming, but deep inside, I felt I was not going to have to attend the course I signed up for, and knew exactly what to do, just like my instructor told me. This is an example of Claircognizance.

Finding the Earring

I was so frustrated. I have a tiny pair of diamond-sapphire dangling earrings, and I couldn't find one of them. I looked everywhere I could think of, but to no avail.

A few days passed, then one night I had a dream and saw the earring below the drawer of a dresser, far from where I stored my jewelry. I remembered the dream the next morning, but at first dismissed it as ridiculous because it was impossible for anything to slip under such a drawer. However, just out of curiosity, I decided to check. I went straight to the middle drawer on the left of the large chest, pulled the heavy drawer out, and lo and behold, there was my tiny earring, right in the middle of the shelf.

How did it get there? It is impossible to place something in that spot unless you deliberately pull out the drawer. How did it come to me in my dream? Do I sleepwalk? This was another strange and helpful dream that gave me a tangible result.

William's Dream

One morning, Naomi's husband William woke up disturbed. He had a vivid dream during the night about his longtime friend John, who lived 3000 miles away. The person in the dream was clearly John, but his facial appearance was totally different. It was as though his face had been "rearranged"—his nose and jaw were substantially altered, and he was covered in scars.

William was quite upset by this vision but decided to dismiss it as a bad dream. The next morning, he went outside to mow the lawn. Inside the house, the phone rang, but Naomi let it go to voice mail. She could hear the message and was shocked. John's wife was calling to inform them that John had been in a terrible accident involving an all-terrain vehicle in a remote mountain area and had to be airlifted out. He would survive and was recuperating; however, his facial bones had been completely crushed and he had undergone multiple surgeries. His skull and face were full of metal plates and his nose and jaw looked quite different.

Naomi immediately ran outside to tell her husband that his dream was true. William initially couldn't believe it, even scoffing at her and telling her it was mean to joke about. So, she played the dramatic voice message for him. They were both in tears over the tragedy, but at the same time amazed at the long-range connection between William and John.

When we sleep, our filters are down, making it easier for us to receive information in real time. Did John contact his close friend William through a dream? All we know is that this is another clear instance of Claircognizance.

Point to Ponder

Have you ever received information about a family member or a close friend via a dream?

CHAPTER 15

Missed Opportunities

We all remember times when we were offered an opportunity to do or have something, and we turned it down. Months or even years later, we realize that it would have been so good for us to follow guidance and accept the gift offered to us then. However, we should not dwell in the past. Sometimes when we miss or ignore Signs, it's because we are not ready.

Near-misses with Shamanism

I had my first opportunity to learn about shamanism during the more than six months I spent living with the Yanomami tribe in the Amazon jungle. The main focus of our work there was to study the plants the shamans were using to heal and bring samples back to an ethnobotany laboratory in Paris for further studies. This gave us the opportunity to directly observe the shamans in their day-to-day activities. However, understanding their processes or tools or even what they did was not on my list of priorities.

Many years later, I had two other opportunities to learn about shamanism, but I still didn't get the Message. Although the Signs were clearly there, I didn't see them at the time.

It wasn't until I was in my late 50s that a medium reminded me that twice, once at age 39 and again at 49, I had turned down opportunities to start on the path of a healer. It took me a while to explore my memories, but I finally realized he was right. There definitely had been Signs I had failed to see. Amazingly, in both cases, they dealt exclusively with shamanism in Korea.

When I was 39, we had just moved to Seoul when I was contacted by someone in the States who worked for the U.S. National Dance Association. She was interested in learning about the history and the status of modern dance in Korea and was wondering if I could write an article for her journal, *Spotlight on Dance*. During my research, as I became acquainted with the Korean dance community, one of the choreographers learned that I was a dancer and invited me to train with her dance company.

Early in the fall of 1988, she invited me to join her dancers on a retreat in the mountains. It was such a privilege and honor; I cannot believe I turned down that fantastic opportunity, but I had a very young child to take care of, and I wasn't comfortable being gone for a week or longer. When the company returned, I learned the retreat was to communicate with Nature and the spirits of Nature. Shamanism is deeply ingrained in Korean society, and it turned out it was a source of inspiration to the choreographer. I will always regret my decision. I would live in Korea for almost two more years. Had I chosen to go, I would have been able to learn so much.

Ten years later, when I was 49, we were back in Korea. Soon after we arrived, I enrolled in a class on shamanism in Korea at the university. I was fascinated by what I learned. What an unbelievable chance I had to be able to attend a private ceremony for a young woman facing difficulties. The "kut" was performed by an old shaman and her two young assistants. In between sections of the rite, we sat around a low table, ate, drank, and talked. I was dying to ask them for permission to attend other ceremonies, but I didn't say anything. One of the assistants spoke good English and was very friendly to me. She seemed to indicate she would like for us to meet again. I can't believe I stayed silent. I regret not accepting her open invitation. I'm sure I could have learned much more with her than in my books; and yet, I missed the Signs once more. Perhaps I didn't pursue it because I was in the process of completing a degree at the university, still had a child at home, and had many other obligations. However, while those were valid reasons, looking back, I know that I missed great opportunities.

I guess I wasn't ready then. It took another decade, when I decided to start learning about energy healing techniques and associated topics, that I embraced shamanic approaches, primarily because my first mentor, with whom I studied for two years, was a shaman. Better late than never.

Point to Ponder

Have you ever had opportunities you didn't pursue and regretted later?

The Printer That Started Itself

Years ago, I was working on my computer late at night in our study when, suddenly, I heard my husband's printer come to life and start printing. My husband was already in bed and his computer was off. Since his printer wasn't connected to my computer, this made me very uncomfortable. I jumped out of my chair and went to see what was happening. The printer was already in the process of printing many copies of the same page, so I stopped it right away. To my great surprise, it was printing a graphic I had used for the cover of a healing course booklet I made a couple of months before. How did it wind up on my husband's printer, and how was that printer started? Too spooked, I quit for the night and went to bed.

The next day, as I was looking intently at the graphic, I saw that it represented the outline of a woman with the Reconnection lines drawn on her body. She was superimposed on top of the earth grid, hiding Europe. Weird! We were in the process of moving from Brussels to the United States. Was this instance of Clairaudience and Clairvoyance as reminder that no matter where I am in the world, nothing will change, and I'll still be connected as usual?

Point to Ponder

Have you ever had an experience you considered strange and, no matter how you look at it, you cannot figure out why it happened?

CHAPTER 16

Warnings

Sometimes, we receive Signs and Messages that we don't understand, only to realize later that the experience was a sort of alert, to tell us to pay attention to something we might be missing. When we need to be on our guard, our Guides and Angels will find a way to let us know.

A Message from Bob Monroe

One evening, my husband and I were in our study. He was reading and I was working on my computer. We were not watching anything on TV, but the screen saver was on and showed an image of planets and the universe. Then, suddenly, the voice of Bob Monroe came through our TV. We were startled. Monroe, who founded the Monroe Institute in the early 1970s, had died in 1995.

When we listened, we realized we were hearing the same message that is at the beginning of all the Monroe Institute's *Human Plus* CD series. We confirmed that none of our computers were connected to the TV and there was no CD playing, and after listening to a few more seconds of the message, my husband turned the TV off entirely. To our surprise, the TV came back on by itself and Bob's voice delivered the exact same message! Again, my husband turned the TV off, and again, a couple minutes later, it came back on, and Bob repeated his message.

What was going on? Once more, we both double-checked all our machines to see if we somehow were connected to the TV. We were not. We were quite puzzled and slightly uncomfortable. My husband suggested I check the CD collection from the Monroe Institute I had beside my desk. The first CD I grabbed was called "Circulation" from the *Human Plus* series. Feeling unsettled, we shut everything down and went to bed.

A couple of days later, I wasn't feeling well and had to go to the doctor. My blood pressure was extremely low, the lowest it had ever been in my life. *It seems to have been a Sign that something was amiss, and I had to check what it was.*

A week later, I was in Paris in my favorite stone and crystal store. Without any prompting or questions from me, the owner took it upon himself to advise me on stones I should wear to improve the blood circulation in my lower limbs.

This series of Synchronicities, which began with the voice of Bob Monroe, was a very strange way for my Guides to get me to pay attention to my blood pressure. I was glad I wasn't alone in the house and that my husband can confirm that we didn't dream it. This instance of Clairaudience remains one of the most unsettling episodes I have ever experienced.

Mysterious Cramps

Our gym in Brussels was a fun place owned by a fantastic trainer. When we returned after a long vacation, there was someone new behind the front desk checking IDs. As soon as I saw him, I felt violent cramps in my stomach. Wondering what was happening, I took a few deep breaths, and the pain lessened a bit. It calmed down during the Body Combat class, but as I was getting ready to leave the gym, I looked at the man and again felt a strong wave of discomfort in my stomach. I just knew there was something evil about him.

The owner of the gym was a friend, so before I left the gym, I asked him who the man was. "My new associate," was the response. He went on to say that this strange man was now in charge of the finances for the business. I received an insight that the man was not there to help my friend, but to rob him. I passed this on right away, but he just laughed at what I said, and I left it at that.

On the way home, I shared what happened with my husband and a neighbor who joined us when we went to the gym. I was still feeling bad in my stomach, and it took a while before I managed to get rid of the discomfort.

About six months later, we received a call very early in the morning from the owner of the gym. He was in shock. When he had arrived at the gym, he discovered that it was almost empty. The door hadn't been forced open, but most of the machines were gone. Someone had come during the night and removed all the newer equipment.

We dashed to the gym; my heart sank when I saw the place bare except for the older machines.

We later learned that the associate was behind the robbery. Worse, since he oversaw the money, most of the money coming in from monthly memberships hadn't been going into the gym's coffers, but into his own account. He also didn't pay the rent for a few months.

My hunch had proven to be right.

I felt bad for my friend, but I had done what I thought was right. My stomach pains were clearly Clairsentience—I could physically feel that something was wrong. I had immediately shared the info I received from the Above, but my friend never believed me. In fact, I frequently receive information to help a friend or someone in need. My Guides let me know that something isn't right and whether I should pass that on.

Point to Ponder

Have you ever received a hunch about something or someone and it later proved to be true?

The Masked Face

One strange Sign I have seen on multiple occasions is a transparent grey mask around a man's eyes. In each instance, I understood right away that it meant danger and acted accordingly. I clearly felt that it was a warning I couldn't ignore.

One evening, when I was a young, single woman, I accepted the invitation of a man I barely knew to have dinner at his place. I should have known better, for I was usually extremely careful. However, that evening, I let my guard down.

The dinner was fine and the discussion interesting—but at one point, I saw a dark shade appear on the upper half of his face, a little bit like a dark, transparent mask. Right away, I experienced shivers going up and down my spine. I knew something was wrong and I had to be very careful.

As a girl living alone in Paris, to stay safe, each time I went out, I always told my neighbor where I was going and with whom. That evening, I felt it was imperative for me to find a way to introduce this information into the conversation, just to let my host know someone knew I was with him and where he lived. Soon afterwards, he got up and left to place a phone call. When he returned, he told me that he was sorry, but he had to go, there was an emergency. I left his place shortly after.

To this day, I wonder what would have happened if I hadn't received this warning from Above. I have seen that dark mask appear again several times during my life—not only in potentially dangerous situations, but also around people I don't know. I take it as a warning Sign and graciously (yet rapidly) keep moving. Clairvoyance and Clairaudience senses were at work here.

Point to Ponder

Have you ever felt extremely uncomfortable when meeting someone for the first time and you couldn't explain why? Did you have a physical reaction as well?

The House That Didn't Want Us

Before we moved to the town where we now live, we spent a lot of time visiting houses around the area. One day, our realtor took us to visit one in a very desirable part of town. The outside looked lovely but as soon as we entered, I felt the atmosphere was very heavy. There was something there that made me feel uncomfortable.

To go from inside the house to the back deck, I slid open the glass door and the screen. The backyard was small but lovely. There was a little creek running into a wooded area. However, when Dave and I decided to go back inside, the screen door was locked. No matter what we did, there was no way to open it. Finally, I noticed a little cut in the screen and made it bigger so I could slide my hand inside. I managed to reach the lock mechanism, which was indeed in the locked position. How did that happen? It added to the uneasiness I had about the place. Still wanting to remain rational, I unlocked the screen and opened it and closed it several more times. Each time, it worked with no problem. There was no reason it should have locked when we were outside. That was very odd.

I had a strange feeling as soon as I entered the house that I now know was a moment of Clairsentience. Although it was in a good location and offered great features, I knew that my hunches were right. There was something there I didn't want to have to deal with. I'm glad we didn't buy that house.

Point to Ponder

Have you ever felt uncomfortable when you entered a house for the first time?

The Tumor in My Thigh

In May 2013, we lived in Brussels. For no apparent reason, I started feeling a lot of pain in my left hip joint. I tried various homeopathic treatments, but it would not go away. Finally, I gave in and went to our GP at the end of July. He was concerned about the possibility of osteoporosis and directed me to get an MRI for both hips. I made an appointment, but the pain went away shortly thereafter so I cancelled it. That was a mistake! Almost immediately after the cancellation, the pain came back with a vengeance, which stopped only when I made a second MRI appointment.

Due to my travelling schedule, I had to delay the scan until late October. When I finally had it, the MRI results showed that I was osteoporosis-free. However, the scan also revealed what appeared to be a massive growth in my upper right thigh. This led to my first visit to Jules Bordet Institute, where I met Dr. Shumelinsky, who determined I had a tumor about the size of a Coke can buried in my thigh muscles.

He told me that I was fortunate; these sorts of rare tumors are often discovered too late, only after they've turned cancerous and extensive damage has already been done. I underwent a major surgery, during which Dr. Shumelinsky spent hours carefully peeling the tumor away from embedded nerve tissues. To this day, I continue to experience some numbness; however, I am cancer-free and able to continue my regular dance/exercise routines.

This series of events includes multiple instances of Clairsentience. Namely, the pain stopped as soon as I made the decision to see my GP, and again when I made an appointment to get an MRI. When I cancelled that appointment, the pain returned immediately. My Guides were doing all they could to let me know it was a pressing matter and I couldn't ignore it.

Point to Ponder

Have you ever ignored pain and discomfort in your body and regretted not having paid attention any sooner?

CHAPTER 17

The Importance of Asking Properly

There was a newly opened bar across the street from our house in Brussels, and it was causing a lot of problems. Our quiet street was noisy almost every night until the wee hours. It wasn't that the patrons of the bar were obnoxious; it's just that, since they couldn't smoke inside the club, they had to go outside—where of course, fueled by alcohol, they would laugh and have loud, animated conversations.

The street's residents placed an official complaint, but to no avail. I decide to step in and use an old, powerful energy technique. I knew the wording had to be chosen very carefully. Instead of directly addressing the situation with the bar, I simply wrote: "May (our street name) be quiet during the day and silent at night." It was a general wish that had nothing out of the ordinary and wasn't formulated to target anyone in particular.

Two months later, the bar filed for bankruptcy and the owner of the building informed me that the next tenant wouldn't be allowed to open a bar. The license to open one was bogus to start with and had just been revoked.

Was my intervention responsible, or would the bar have lost its license regardless? I will never know. I will also not feel guilty, knowing I simply asked for the street to be silent at night, and never wished any harm to the bar or its owners.

The Antidote to Pain Is Love

When we decided to retire to the U.S. in 2013, we needed to sell our Brussels house. Our home was a very beautiful, late 19th century townhouse with a little garden and even a secret room hidden behind the library walls, located in a very desirable location in the center of Brussels. All the required upgrades and inspections had been completed, so we expected a quick sale.

Unfortunately, for over a year we experienced one bureaucratic nightmare after another. There was always something that prevented us from receiving the final agreement from the commune (city government) we lived in. Our notary told us he had never seen that sort of situation before. He couldn't understand what was going on because we had done everything normally required.

A man had agreed to buy our home and was renting it and living there while he waited for the government to allow us to sell it. But we were afraid that after so many months, he would get tired of waiting and walk away. My husband and I had already moved to our new home in the States, and every day I would wake up dreading another email of complaint from the tenant or demand from the commune issued via the notary.

I finally realized that I should investigate at another level. I started researching energetically to see if something unusual might be happening. I had a feeling that someone was blocking the sale, but I didn't want to accuse anyone and preferred to contact two mediums, friends of mine in France and the U.S., before taking any action. They both determined that what I already suspected was the answer—someone was, knowingly or unknowingly, blocking the sale. This confirmed my suspicions about a particular individual, although I chose to believe that she was doing it unknowingly. I know from experience that it's possible to emit a very strong negative energy when in pain.

I knew this person had lived a very difficult life and was in need of a lot of love. So, I decided the best way to resolve the problem was to send her the love she needed. Each day, after my meditation, I sent love her way. I can't say it was very easy at first, but it gradually became easier to do.

I went to France about two months later and met her. Even though I had known her for about 20 years, she never had been as kind towards me as she was this time. She was a different person. I cautiously waited for her to revert to her old ways, but she never did. To this day, she is a delightful person to know. Plus, about three months after I started to send her love, all the problems surrounding the sale of our home disappeared. The commune finally issued the certificate we needed, and the tenant was able to sign the sales agreement.

Would the sale have gone through when it did without any intervention on my part? I don't know. But to see this woman become a different person entirely after sending her positive loving energy for a few weeks is something I can't explain. It actually helped me a lot too, because it forced me to get over my conflicted feelings about her and allowed me to grow in consciousness.

Part 3

D o you ever wonder why Synchronicity seems to happen to some people, but not to you? This section will help you determine what might be holding you back and, even better, move past the block and connect with your own Guides and Angels.

Don't worry, I promise it's easy (well, with a bit of effort)! Just change your attitude and the Winks from Above will appear to you, too.

CHAPTER 18

Blocks

What prevents us from seeing the Signs and connecting with our Guides? Several times in my life—sometimes for long periods—I have not been able to access my Guides. Yes, they were still there, but I couldn't sense them or acknowledge their presence. I let "issues," externally or internally induced, keep them behind the Veil.

Our Guides are always present, ready to communicate with us. Whether we do or not is up to us. If we keep our heart open to the Signs and Synchronicities they place on our path, we succeed in receiving their Messages, and in doing so, we obtain the resources we need to help us navigate our life path. But if we close our heart, we miss the opportunity to see, interpret, accept, and use those Messages.

Communication Breakdown

Sometimes communication with our Guides is cut—not because they give up and stop watching over us, but because we are incapable of receiving their Messages. This happens:

- When our heart is so full of anger and hatred, it's closed. No light can get in, we are blind and deaf.
- When our heart is so full of fear, we become petrified. We can't move in any direction except retreat deeper into our comfort zone.
- When our heart is so full of sorrow, it's engrossed in soothing its own pain and no sensation of connection with our Guides is possible. We are numb.
- When our heart is incapable of love towards ourselves, our daily life is full of misery. Failure is always waiting.
- When our heart is so full of ourselves, no matter what our Guides try to convey, we look down on it. We may see the Signs, but our misguided sense of pride leads us to believe that we know better.
- When our heart understands the Messages, but we feel that the action required is too hard, too much has to be changed, it's too inconvenient or a new path seems too difficult to follow. We do nothing.
- When in our heart, we don't believe anything outside what we have learned through the teaching of our parents, the school, the church and/or our friends, we are blocked from taking the necessary steps to move forward on our life path. Our journey becomes singularly linear. No matter what happens, we will not venture on a new path, even if it leads to a better way for us to reach the end of our journey.

All the above block the Guiding Light, the Signs, the Messages to reach not only our heart but also our intuition and our inner voice. Our intuition is what connects us with our Guides and Angels on the other side of the Veil.

Procrastination

There are many different, often profound reasons for procrastination. Unfortunately, regardless of the reason, procrastination doesn't lead anywhere except to frustration, low self-esteem and sometimes even depression. It prevents the flow of creativity, which isn't conducive to opening up so we can see and receive Signs from Above. Messages from our Guides are often missed or misinterpreted, or worse, we see them but feel too lazy to follow their lead. We remind ourselves to get to it "someday…"

Self-doubt/Impostor Syndrome

When we feel inadequate and unworthy, it's very difficult to trust our intuition. When we don't love and don't believe in ourselves, even if we see and are able to interpret the Signs, we can't believe our good fortune. We don't believe we deserve what's offered to us and we won't listen to what our voice of wisdom is telling us.

Depression

When we are so full of anguish or sorrow, and we feel helpless in front of the challenges we face, we might fall into depression. This creates a thick grey cloud between us and our Guides. No matter how many Signs are placed on our path, how many Messages we receive through our intuition, dreams, etc., no light can come through and we remain impervious to what our Guides are trying to tell us.

Although I couldn't have explained it then, this is exactly what I experienced when I had depression. It felt like, for a long period, the light guiding me on my path faded to nothingness. I realized later I was going through the "growing pains" of becoming aware that I was more than my physical body. This period of transition wasn't easy, but even though I couldn't see where I was going for a while, I gradually rediscovered all the necessary tools to progress. My major depression was not only the end of that cycle, it also was the beginning of an incredible, productive new phase.

Focusing on the Past or the Future

It's important to remember to keep our mind, our heart, our whole being open. This is difficult to maintain if we continue to relive our past or project ourselves into a bleak, imagined future. In both cases, it will, most of the time, lead us into a place of regret, anger, or yearning for what never was or never will be. *The present* is where we are able to walk with serenity in our heart. Staying present and in the present helps alleviate the burden we carry when navigating a difficult period. The change may not be apparent right away, but it will lighten the weight we have in our hearts. It will also foster a heightened sense of hope and help us see the Signs, sense the presence of our Guides and Angels, and ease the pain we are experiencing.

This does not mean we won't have to experience pain. It's just that spending time in the present will let us find respite and a sense of peace, easing that pain, at least for a while. Being in the present isn't about focusing on the pain we're experiencing, instead it's focusing our attention and our energy on what we see, what we feel, what we hear, and what our intuition is telling us at that moment. This heightened awareness can divert us from our pain, even if it's excruciating, for a brief period.

More importantly, the more we slip back into the past or project ourselves into the future without considering what the present is telling us, the more it's bound to blind us to whatever is placed in our path. It keeps us prisoner. We are trapped in our own lower self. Remember, we are more than what we think we are. We are beings of light, and to keep our light shining bright, we need to be in the present. When faced with adversity, rather than let our light become dim, we must strive to keep it shining bright. It's necessary to become and remain a beacon of peace and hope to others.

Fear

Following Divine guidance isn't always comfortable. It sometimes requires courage to get out of our comfort zone and have the strength to change our path so that we can shift to move in an unfamiliar direction. A dramatic change can be exciting but also very scary. The unknown often is. And sometimes, that fear can get in the way. Someone made a very clever acronym with the word: **F**alse **E**vidence **A**ppearing **R**eal. As long as we're under the grip of fear, believing that false evidence, it's very difficult to clearly see what steps need to be taken to make changes. Our inner wisdom and our Spirit Guides are tuned out. Our guiding light is very dim or off.

Hatred and/or Anger

When we are full of hatred or anger, we're enveloped by the same kind of thick grey cloud that wraps around us during depression. We are so disturbed by our strong negative emotions that it becomes impossible to think with clarity. It makes us blind and deaf, rendering us incapable of seeing Signs and understanding Messages. While we have still not been abandoned by our Guides and Angels, we cannot feel their loving presence and guidance.

Negativity

Negativity begets negativity. This state of mind shades everything we do with darkness and closes our being, our soul, to any connection with our Guides and Angels. Signs and Messages are either not seen or are misinterpreted in a negative way. We can't avoid having bad days altogether, but we owe it to ourselves to keep our distance from negative people.

Preconceived Notions

A preconceived idea of how a Sign will appear might prevent us from seeing it altogether. Signs and Messages show up in so many different forms. It could be a word, a repetition of numbers, an animal, a situation, an association of ideas, an encounter, etc. If you expect Signs to take a specific form, you might miss them, either partially or entirely. So, it's essential to keep a very open mind and heart. Also, remember that imagination is a very powerful tool and is often needed to help us interpret what we see.

Lack of Flexibility

Sometimes it can feel like it's too hard to change the course of our life. It demands too many sacrifices, and sometimes, it takes courage to accept changes. The road to reach our goals isn't always a straight path. Many hurdles and unexpected events prevent us from going all the way to the end. Even when Signs are clear and easily understood, the realization of what it would take to reach what we desire is scary. We don't want to go down that path and we keep finding reasons why we shouldn't. So, we don't.

Setbacks

A promotion we don't get, a friend who disappears from our lives, an unexpected illness, etc. All of these can make us feel abandoned by the Universe and our Spirit Guides. It's normal to feel disappointed, sad, or scared when faced with such situations. However, when the initial disappointment and pain subside, we can have a better vision of what the unwanted event means.

A promotion not attained might prepare us for a better position, another opportunity. A friendship that fades away might not be useful or appropriate in our life anymore. An illness might indicate an underlying condition, physical or even sometimes emotional.

Like when my husband and I lost the dream home we were planning to buy, only to find a better one for us. Sometimes a disappointment is just opening the door to an even more desirable opportunity.

BLOCKS

Only when we open our heart to all possibilities can we see the many Signs our Guides place before us. Only then are their Messages visible to us so we can understand them and take action as necessary.

CHAPTER 19

Inviting Synchronicity

Throughout my life, I've developed several helpful ways to enhance my ability to see Signs, interpret them, and take action. In the following passages, I will highlight some of these approaches through several examples pulled from my personal experiences. They've worked for me, and they might be thought-provoking and useful for you too.

In addition, as an aid for those of you who might be interested, I have also included a few exercises and meditations. I've found these to be quite helpful to open, reopen, or keep open, my senses, both physical and "clair," so I can receive the Signs around me. There are many ways to help ourselves remain balanced and prevent a gray mist from surrounding us. The little list below is by no means the only way to help reach clarity, openness, balance, and happiness in your life, but I do hope it helps.

Dance-Meditation

In the morning, I love to dance before I meditate. I discovered this by accident. One day, I turned on what I thought was meditation music when it was, in fact, lively dance music. I swayed and moved to the strong rhythm for the five minutes it lasted. I felt so good when it stopped! My whole body was buzzing, and the inner turmoil I experienced earlier that morning was gone. After I sat down, it was easy to get into a meditative state. No more chatting monkeys in my brain, just peace. Since then, I usually combine dance and meditation. It often brings fantastic insights into what I'm going through, or sometimes a new creative idea pops up out of nowhere. I keep a pad and pen close by so I can jot down what comes to my mind.

Exercise

Yes, I am asking you to dance and meditate. While I am a dancer, I promise there is no need to be a trained dancer to do this. Just find a moment alone and let the music be the vehicle to reach whatever is going on inside you. Then move in a way that feels good and right to you. Remember, nobody is watching you!

If you're angry, unsettled, or in a dark place, choose a dynamic beat like hard rock music and do whatever movements help you expel your negative energy like stomping your feet, jumping, kicking, punching, etc. You might even add vocalization to help get rid of what's weighing on you. If you're not in a hard-rock mood, you can also listen to any song or instrumental or ambient music and let it take over and inspire you to move in fluid motion.

For those who prefer, it's possible to internalize the rhythm while standing still or even sitting. Whatever position you choose, the point is to feel the music flow and vibrate through you.

Close your eyes, let the music invade your whole being and let any body parts or your entire body move and enjoy the moment. Again, nobody is watching you.

Enjoy a few minutes of abandonment. Joy, anger, sorrow can come out. Just let them surface and then evaporate. After a few minutes, very little tension will be left to interfere with your meditation.

If you happen to dance-meditate outside, you could forego the music and instead just listen to Nature's melody. The beautiful sounds of the birds, the light wind in the branches, or the sound of the waves can soothe, inspire, and go straight to your soul.

Whenever possible, I love to be on the beach at sunrise, where I can dance near the water and run, jump, stomp and kick the small waves. It makes this 72-year-old feel like a little child without a worry in the world. I usually end up laughing and squealing with joy!

Gratitude

There is an exercise I like to use when I wake up, especially when I feel some uneasiness about something I can't put my finger on. It's a two-page side-by-side assessment that can be virtual or written down. Sometimes, I do it even before getting out of bed. Here's how it works:

Exercise

- On the left page, I visualize or write down all the positive things in my life I should be thankful for. Family, job, health, talents, friends, etc. I even list the little things that make me happy. It's typically quite a long list.

- The right page is for all that is wrong in my life. Even though life is never perfect, I find that once I write down the list of grievances and then take a moment to consider their impact, many of them suddenly diminish or disappear.

As a result, only a few things or none remain for me to gripe about. Of course, major trauma such as death, divorce, etc., require a different approach. However, when I wake up feeling less than perfect, this little exercise helps me start the day on a more positive and solid footing. It gives me the perspective that, after all, I have it pretty good. My heart is full of gratitude.

Active Meditation

When I don't need to do the above gratitude ritual, I like to start meditating by being thankful in general for what I have. It opens my whole being and puts me in a more receptive place to let peace enter my soul.

Exercise

In addition to starting my meditation by dancing, I sometimes end it by sending distance healing towards a person or a group of people who need help. For the latter, I follow these steps:

1. I stand or sit in the direction of the rising sun.
2. I place my left hand, palm up and parallel to the ground, at the level of my heart. Then, I put my right hand, palm down, above it, as if I were holding a precious crystal.

3. I visualize that shiny crystal and see it grow bigger and brighter until it reaches the size of a huge, brilliant, white balloon.

4. I infuse it with my intentions (like love or healing) and send it as I would send a beach ball in the direction of the person or people who need love or healing.

5. Sometimes I hold the large balloon in my hands in front of my face and blow on it, sending it away with kisses.

This is the technique I used with the person I suspected was blocking the sale of our house. I knew that she was in pain, which caused her to act in ways that were detrimental to others, and I understood her suffering had to be addressed. So, I did what I explained above and sent her a balloon filled with love. To my delight, when I saw her a few weeks later, she was a different person. That experience has empowered me to use this technique over and over. Not only does it help whoever is the recipient, but it also helps me and makes me feel very good.

Of course, you can develop your own method rather than the one described above. Just do whatever is comfortable so that you can send what the person needs. Your intention is the key, and it's a very powerful tool.

Once the thought or wish is sent toward the recipient, the feeling of love you'll experience is exhilarating.

Ways to Connect with Your Spirit Guides

- **Be Aware of the Synchronicities in Your Life**

  Open your eyes and your mind's eye, especially when you're experiencing a challenging or an important period of your life and you need guidance. You'll notice a link, a thread between events that seem unrelated at first. To do so might bring clarity. Because the information is so valuable, it's a good idea to keep a journal of Synchronicities.

- **Remain Open but Grounded**

  When you see Signs, don't be obsessed and try to find every single meaning. When your mind is open and your body relaxed, you'll effortlessly get the Message, and it might be very different from the one you would have perceived if you tried to dissect it. Remember that Guides and Angels are walking beside you to provide help when you need it. That should allow you to relax knowing that you're surrounded by loving entities.

- **Via Dreams**

Exercise

1. Before going to bed, mentally ask your Guides and Angels for assistance and guidance regarding a problem you need help with. Or write it down on a piece of paper and place it on your bedside table or under your pillow. Keep the request short and simple.

2. As you're falling asleep, silently repeat your request over and over.

3. Keep a pen and paper near you to jot down (if you can) whatever comes through your dreams. You might get exactly the answer you need. Or it might suddenly come to you the next day.

Stay True to Yourself

When we entered this life, we still, at first, remained connected. There was no separation between this dimension and the other. As we grew up, that separation increased until we stopped connecting with our Guides and Angels and forgot where we came from.

Some inculcated beliefs make many people believe that they are connected. While they may be in some way, multiple layers of falsehood might often mask their true essence. The Signs and Messages they receive from Above might be misinterpreted. The key is to remain true to ourselves and keep our inner child alive and present—the purity of their heart is your true essence. Reconnect with it. It's where your power is. Your inner child knows more than you think. Let them lead you to see life through their eyes. Let them help you enjoy the simpler things in life. Let them guide your heart to appreciate what's placed on your path.

With an open mind, you'll see beauty where there is ugliness. You'll see goodness in the heart of people even if they don't see it themselves. You'll see humor and beauty in many instances when others see nothing. A star, a voice, the beautiful song of a bird, a sudden refreshing breeze caressing your face, wonderment in the eyes of a child looking up at you, the presence of a loved one—all of these will become daily Winks from Above in your life.

Exercise

Today, open to your inner child and try to see, hear, or sense a Wink placed on your path. How does it make you feel?

Share Positivity and Inner Joy

Once, in a supermarket, I was waiting in line to pay for my purchases. I noticed the cashier did not have a very agreeable appearance, and her angry expression was not helping. I was trying very hard to find something to say to lift her spirits as the shortening line brought me closer to the register. But nothing was coming to my mind. When I was in front of her, ready to pay, I noticed she was wearing a brooch— nothing that I would wear, but very interesting and unusual, nonetheless. I said with a smile, "What an interesting and lovely brooch you have." She seemed to come out of her daze. Her facial contours softened, and she said, "Thank you!" with a smile. That smile made her look pretty. As I left, I checked and noticed that she was still wearing that smile while attending to the person behind me. Mission accomplished! It made me feel so good. When I left the store, I was floating and sensed my Guides were cheering.

Another time, I was in the metro in Paris, seated in front of a woman who was talking on her phone. The noise was such that I couldn't hear what she said, but her body language indicated she was dealing with a difficult situation. She hung up and called someone else. It was apparent that this, too, was an unpleasant conversation. She hung up and made another call. The calls back and forth seemed to be to two people who were disagreeing, and she was the go-between. Finally, she put her phone away, clearly very perturbed. The metro had just come out above ground and was now rolling outside under a brilliant sun. I don't know why, but suddenly I leaned forward, gently took her hands in mine, looked into her eyes, and said with a smile, "And now it's time to breathe." She looked at me, surprised, paused for a second, and said, "You're right. I used to do yoga." Since it was lunchtime, I suggested that if she had time, a short walk in the sun might help. We got off at the same station and she told me she was going to walk outside. She thanked me and said she wished more people would do what I had just done. It really helped her. I smiled and told her to pass it on. I walked away feeling like I was riding on a little cloud. I not only helped her, but I also received so much joy in return.

This encounter put me in a place that was very conducive to seeing Signs and understanding what my Guides were trying to share with me.

Exercise

Follow your intuition and provide a smile or a kind word to someone you feel needs it.

Maybe your Guides are asking you to transmit a message of love to someone in need. Be careful not to force yourself, or it might seem out of place and awkward. Wait for the moment when, deep inside, you feel someone's pain. Then let your smile come from your heart, and the right words will appear. Try it. It brings so much joy and makes you walk taller afterward. I know it always does for me.

Build a Vision Board

An excellent way to make your visions or dreams more tangible is to create a Vision (Dream) Board. I'll describe the basic principle for those not familiar with this way of manifesting your intentions. You can also go on the internet and find all kinds of ideas, patterns, and styles. Here is a basic, step-by-step plan:

Exercise

1. First, make a list of all the visions/dreams you have for a specific project and for a definite period of time.

2. Gather the material you'll need: a poster board, crayons, felt pens, old magazines, photos, mementos, stickers, scissors, glue, tape.
3. Browse through the magazines and cut out the pictures or words you're interested in. You can also look online for specific pictures or words you have in mind and print them.
4. Start placing the pictures and words on the board in a way that is visually appealing to you. It's important that wherever you place an item, it attracts your eye and reminds you daily of your important goals.
5. Make sure your vision/dream board is in a place where you can see it throughout the day. It will become a good reminder of what you really want and help you work toward your goals.

Positive Thinking

Negativity begets negativity. It's essential to keep a positive attitude when facing challenges. I'm not saying it's always possible, but there are many cases during which a little bit of humor goes a long way.

Here are three examples I used during my month-long recovery stay at the hospital.

- I was on the top floor of the hospital building in a private room with a huge, wall-to-wall bay window. When it was windy, the outside shutters made a lot of noise. One day, it was particularly windy, and no one could come right away to fix a couple of shutters that had come partially unattached. I had the choice to be miserable because of the rattling or to use it to my advantage. I closed my eyes, and the noise suddenly reminded me of a sailboat with big sails flapping in the wind. So, I decided to be on a boat sailing from my bed in Brussels to exotic shores under a beautiful warm sun. The doctors and nurses who attended me had fun when they asked if I was bothered by the noise, and I told them to close their eyes and imagine themselves joining me on "my" sailboat. They did, and it made them smile.

- Dealing with a feeding tube for 29 days straight wasn't the most comfortable way to eat. Immediately after my operation, a tube was inserted into my right nostril and pushed all the way down into my stomach, and for almost a month, all my nourishment came from feeding pouches. The hospital staff or visitors would ask me if I was bothered by the fact that I couldn't put anything in my mouth or taste anything. I told them that it's very simple. At "mealtime," I can decide what gourmet dish to have and be very fancy and demanding at no extra cost. I would simply close my eyes and imagine I was enjoying any of a number of tantalizing foods. Lobster bisque was one of my favorites!

193

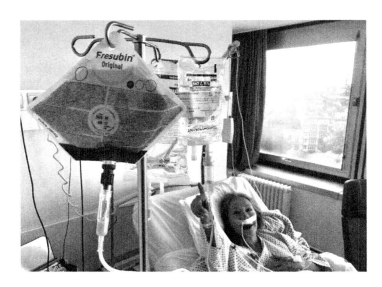

For 29 days, the feeding pouches became my "daily buffet."

- Having a CT scan or an MRI is not a favorite procedure for anyone. I found a way to make it not only bearable but also (almost) enjoyable. As I'm pushed into the bright cylinder, I close my eyes and imagine myself lounging comfortably on the deck of a boat. The sun is very bright and warm, and I can actually feel it above me. The sky is bright blue—I even hear a seagull nearby. When I begin to feel the vibration of the motor and hear the loud, rhythmic pounding sound of the machine, I imagine it as the boat, picking up speed as it enters high seas. I usually get so relaxed that one time, I even fell asleep. The key is to never open my eyes because then, the magic just disappears.

I love to close my eyes and use images. It sometimes helps a great deal when I have no control over a temporarily unpleasant situation. The examples above can be slightly adjusted and applied to many other situations. Ah! The power of unbound imagination!

Exercise

Your turn now! The next time you're faced with a disagreeable (yet temporary!) situation, and you have no control over it, let your imagination step in and create a different scenario.

Pay Attention

It's not always easy to stay in the present, but it's essential. True, when the present is temporarily unpleasant, I use my imagination to alter reality (see above). But that's not the kind of disconnect I'm referring to here. I'm talking about those times we internally disconnect from our true selves by projecting ourselves into unpleasant past events or scary future scenarios. This is when we must remember to come back and stay in the present—and pay attention. That's when the magic can happen. Then it becomes easier to see Signs and perceive the Messages our Guides are trying to convey with more clarity.

It's equally important as we do this to open our hearts. That's when the Signs and Messages placed in front of us can be clearly seen, interpreted, and used without interference.

Exercise

The next time you catch yourself reliving painful past events or imagining frightening future scenarios, make a conscious effort to come back to the present—to center yourself. Take a few deep, controlled breaths, go for a short walk, work out, or listen to music. It might be all you need to help you snap out of the negative mode you're in.

Walking in the Present

Signs are always with you. Let everything in Nature talk to your heart. It might bring clarity if you are confused or give you the answer you have been looking for. Just listen, see, feel—sense the Messages. Your whole being might receive them in a way you are not used to experiencing. Your sense of smell will be heightened, your eyes will see further, your ears will be attuned to the faintest sound, your heart will be filled with gratitude. You might even reach a point when the line between your human senses and your intuitive senses blurs. Do you see with your human eyes or your mind's eye? Do you hear with your human ears or your mind's ear?

Open your heart to all the possibilities. That's when all the Signs placed in front of you can be seen and you can hear the guidance. The Messages, *all* the Messages, will be visible, perceived, and understood.

A friend who was also studying energy healing in Paris went to the Pyrenees in the South of France during her Summer vacations. One day, as she was hiking in the mountains, she heard a little voice calling. She ignored it at first, thinking it was in her head. But it kept calling. After a few minutes, she decided to search out the source of that strange little voice. She discovered it was coming from a tiny flower. She cut one as a sample so she could check at the library to find out what kind of flower it was. She discovered that that plant had been used for healing during the Middle Ages. It motivated her to study plants intensively, and she began crafting essential oils in the traditional way. It added another tool to her healer's bag.

Meditating during a silent stroll through the woods, on a beach, or in the mountains allows us to listen not only to the beautiful and peaceful sounds of Nature, but also to our soul. This can provide an excellent opening to receive guidance and Messages from Above. The channel becomes wide open.

Exercise

Take a walk in Nature and be in the moment with each element, one at a time.

1. Listen to your steps. What sounds do they make in the grass? On dry leaves? In the snow?
2. Listen to the trickling from an invisible brook or a river nearby. Does it sing to you?
3. Smell the rich fragrance from the forest after the rain. Do you feel grounded?
4. Listen to your breath. Is it deep? Shallow? Fast? Slow?
5. Listen to the wind. Is it playful? Teasing?
6. Feel the soft breeze on your face during your walk. Is it cool? Warm? Refreshing?
7. Listen to the birds. What songs are they singing? Are they flying or perched nearby? Can you see them?
8. Look at the sky through the tall branches of the magnificent trees. Is it clear blue? Cloudy and gray?
9. Feel your heart and open to your inner voice. Can you sense the wonders of Nature?

If you are walking with other people, let them know you're not ignoring them but that you just need to be silent for a while. This allows you to be in a meditative state even while others are nearby. You will find that with a little practice, you can ignore any conversations that otherwise might prove distracting.

Be in Silence

We live in a world of constant noise and agitation. However, many of us feel lonely, down, or just off-center when in total silence. It's not unusual for someone to turn on the TV or play music to feel less alone.

However, while some types of music may be great ways to elevate our mood, constant music isn't necessarily healthy. It can be parasitic to the mind and prevent us from thinking freely. Being swayed by sounds to act or feel a certain way impedes the freedom to let our thoughts flow.

I'm not saying that music, in general, is not a good thing. It can lift our spirits or help us reach mental states that are very desirable. However, sometimes, when all is still, thoughts from deep inside can come forth in a clearer way and not be drowned out by distracting sounds.

Besides, total silence doesn't really exist. If we pay attention, the wind, the waves, the rain, the birds, the cars, the ticking of the clock are sounds that surround us. Here is a little exercise I like to do when I need to go deep inside myself.

Exercise

1. Listen for the sounds that are the furthest away from where you are. They might be cars on a highway a mile away, planes flying above…
2. Bring your attention closer to you, a few streets away or maybe a half-mile away. It could be trains, trucks, klaxons, construction work…
3. Your attention is now on your street, close to where you live. You might hear voices of people passing by, children playing, a car coming down the road, crows cawing, a dog barking, a strong howling wind, someone mowing a lawn, heavy rain…
4. Now, pay attention to what's happening inside your home. A clock is ticking, someone is on the phone in another room, the cat is meowing, the HVAC unit turns on…
5. Now, bring your attention to your inner self—that's when your mind's ear and eye take over.
6. Listen to and feel your heartbeat.

7. Listen to and feel your breathing; visualize your breath coming in and out of your lungs.

8. Continue breathing slowly and deeply until you can feel/see yourself entering a beautiful, brilliant white space where you observe your physical self gradually disappearing as you merge into this new environment. You are weightless and in a beautiful state of suspension.

You are now one with All That Is, where you can refresh and rejuvenate. All the channels are now open, and you can interact with your Guides and Angels.

Angel Numbers

I think of Angel Numbers as little Winks from Above. They are reminders throughout my day that I'm not alone. Each number has a meaning, but I don't always check all the details. I just know that someone from the other realm is watching over me, and this alone is comforting. The Messages conveyed by the numbers are never negative. They simply offer encouragement or more information about where to focus my attention.

The list of numbers and their combinations is too long to give here; just keep in mind that these numbers are Messages from your Spirit Guides. There is a lot written about the number combinations, but this is not the place to describe in detail what they all mean. If you're curious, go on the internet or buy a book to get all the specifics. The most important thing to remember right now is that when you see a number repeatedly, check its meaning because it's a Sign that someone from the invisible realm is trying to communicate with you. This technique is beneficial when you're lost and unsure of what to do next. I see these numbers constantly and feel they are Signs my Spirit Guides place on my path throughout the day and I'm very grateful. Those little Winks often make me smile.

Exercise

When you notice repeating numbers, record them in a journal.

Additionally, if anything in your life keeps repeating, investigate its meaning. A repeating word is probably straightforward. If it's a piece of music, check the title or tune in to find out how you feel each time it plays. A color or a pattern you see everywhere might be a bit more difficult to interpret, but it might have a significant meaning to *you*. Anything that appears over and over in your life for no apparent reason is always worth checking. Bumping into the same person, again and again, might also be worth a look into why it's happening.

Record any repeating words, sounds, patterns, colors, or anything that keeps appearing in your life in a journal.

Adopt the Heart of a Child

As I'm writing this book, I have the luck to spend time with our two-and-a-half-year-old granddaughter several times a week. To look at the expression of wonderment and the glee in her eyes warms my heart. This ability to find beauty and happiness in the simplest things is still within all of us, but it's buried under the many layers of years of adulthood. The way my granddaughter discovers and explores her environment is such a delight and a reminder of how to look and revel again at all that surrounds us. It helps me to rekindle the excitement of looking, listening, tasting, and touching that I have taken for granted most of my adult life. Simple joys abound. We just have to let them come into full view.

I can still surprise myself when I discover that I'm singing to my house plants or apologizing to a flower I need to remove or cut. I find it helpful when I have to trim a bush to ask it to guide my hands to where I should or can cut it. People say that I have a green thumb, but I believe it's simply because I appreciate and respect everything animate and inanimate in Nature and seek their counsel whenever possible.

The key to being able to increase our ability to see and interpret Signs, as well as to connect with our Spirit Guides, is to be open, relaxed, and curious, just like a child. That innate, even innocent quality is still there within all of us, even though it may be buried under decades of "adult" thinking and "real world" challenges.

Going for a walk down our street with our granddaughter takes a long time, as we must stop at every interesting bug, seed, twig, leaf, flower, or pebble on our way. I don't mind following her and rejoice at everything she picks up, admires, and makes comments on. It teaches me to appreciate once again those little things that are readily available and that our adult eyes don't see anymore. During our walks, she is my little guide.

It's during such peaceful times that our soul opens fully, our creative mind is alert, and our intuition is at its best. It's easier to see and interpret Signs when our boundaries are expanded. A tiny, flying bug can lead to a universe we're not familiar with. A pebble to the immensity of the sea. A flower to an outpouring of love.

Viewing different elements with fresh eyes, ears, and hearts can lead to thoughts that often have nothing to do with the original stimulus. For instance, a scent might bring a color; a color might bring a sound; an event might bring a shape; or a sound might bring a person. They're all intermingled. When our mind is at rest and our spirit free to soar, what was dim or out of sight before might appear in full view and with clarity.

We adults tend to overthink and get lost while overanalyzing a Sign. It's not always a bad thing, but sometimes having the spontaneity of a child helps us learn while remaining in touch with our true self.

When I was in the Dance Academy in Paris, I was doing very well. However, after I successfully passed one of my exams, my Dance Master told me he thought I could go even further; that I was still missing a little something. After our discussion and much soul searching, I realized that I lacked spontaneity in my learning approach. I would constantly analyze every movement, the reaction in my body, and how I could hone my skills by improving my body's performance. It was an excellent approach for moving forward and developing a powerful and precise instrument, but I needed to add joy and fun to what I was doing. The best way to do that was to learn just like a child does. No analysis—just see, do, and have fun. Be spontaneous! Forget the process; just move and enjoy it. Once my muscles had internalized the movement, it was possible to work on the needed precision.

Dance improvisation allowed me to gradually get back in touch with my inner child. That was decades ago, but to this day, my dancing before my morning meditation often allows me to reconnect with the child within.

Follow your inner child. Their heart is pure, they are wise and their knowledge greater than you can imagine. That is where you can find your true essence. Your inner child is never tainted by human drama.

Have you ever felt that it would be fun to do something or act a certain way, but you decided against it because you thought you were too old? The next time, why not let the child within guide you and have fun?

Exercise

Follow your inner child the next time you're prompted to do something you usually might consider childish, a bit silly, or not age-appropriate. How do you feel afterwards?

Read Your Diaries

Looking back over your life might reveal a wealth of information hidden between the pages. I know it did for me.

Pay attention when you come across words like *weird, strange, bizarre, unusual, unbelievable, scary,* and the like. They could well indicate that your story, your anecdote, falls into one of the categories I described in Part Two of this book. You may have seen Signs or had encounters or been exposed to opportunities you didn't understand or even realize at the time.

To write this book, I had to do this exercise myself. I was amazed to discover that so many of the stories I had dismissed as strange can now actually be explained with the knowledge and understanding I have acquired since they happened. The more of these "red flags" I found, the more they brought forth memories of other unusual happenings I had totally forgotten.

It was so comforting to find out that even during the darkest periods of my life, when I was spiritually "challenged" and my whole being was impervious to any stimuli, I was never alone. My Guides and Angels were tirelessly trying to attract my attention by placing many Winks from Above on my path.

Exercise

Keep a journal/diary to record events you rediscover in old diaries and add the ones you're going to notice from now on.

Conclusion

The experience of being guided through my illness to what was an ultimately positive outcome was a catalyst for me. Knowing how much my own connection to the Above had helped me, I felt compelled to share everything I knew to encourage people to reconnect with their Spirit Guides and innate abilities to see and interpret the Signs placed in their path.

This process required me to go back in time and try to remember all the significant events I needed to mention to illustrate what I wanted to convey. In order to interpret my experiences and explain the process of connecting with the Above as clearly as possible, I also had to do a lot of research. Assessing the most pivotal events of my life through this new lens brought a lot of clarity to memories that were previously vague. I rediscovered so much that had been kept secret between the pages of old diaries, bringing back memories of long-forgotten, interesting stories and allowing for more to resurface. It was a wonderful trip down memory lane.

Some of the stories were a bit difficult to revisit because they happened during a painful time in my life. Yet, looking at them through the filter of knowledge I have acquired since they happened, I felt detached and able to face them. This allowed for discoveries pertinent to what I hoped to explain in this book. Meaning that while I started this project wanting to help others, in fact, I received a lot of help too.

On that note, let me again encourage you to write down any memories that come to mind and see if you can figure out which of the intuitive or Clair-senses was at play during each of those events. I also hope you will keep in mind some of the "Points to Ponder" and try a few of the "Exercises" in this book, as I am confident that at least some of them will help you gradually reconnect with your Spirit Guides and reclaim the abilities you were born with.

My goal for this book is that, by noticing all the help that our Spirit Guides provide us, we can all feel empowered to walk more clearly and confidently on our life path. Some of this guidance is designed to help us through life's most serious moments, others are there to help us rediscover and embrace our inner child. All these strange, bizarre, inexplicable, weird, fascinating, exciting, and even just plain interesting moments are meant to remind us that we are more than our physical body and demonstrate that we are never alone. They are our daily little miracles—our Winks from Above.

Glossary of Key Terms

(NOTE: These are not formal definitions. Rather, they are descriptions of terms, or related to terms, I use throughout this book to explain important entities and activities related to seeing, interpreting, and using Signs in our daily lives.)

Animal Spirits

Animal Spirits are often divided into several types:

1. "Life" Spirit Animal – a person's primary Guide throughout life; often an animal they are drawn to as a child or one that appears in dreams.

2. "Journey" Spirit Animal – appears at points when a major, life-changing decision must be made.

3. "Messenger" Spirit Animal – alerts the person to a specific situation.

4. "Shadow" Spirit Animal– serves to test the person, to teach them that certain habits or attitudes need to be changed.

Ascended Masters

Beings who were once human and have completed the karmic cycle and ascended, yet have elected to remain available to help other humans by applying the knowledge and experience they've gained during their own journeys to help guide us through the ascension processes.

Astral Projection
A form of OBE (out-of-body experience) in which a person experiences the sensation of departing from their physical body while retaining consciousness. This is an intentional experience that occurs when a person deliberately sends their consciousness out of their body toward a different physical location or even dimension. (See also OBE.)

Channeling
Channeling occurs when a Spirit Guide or other Higher Being uses a person to communicate specific information to another person or persons. Interestingly, the person channeling is typically not aware of being used in this manner and has no knowledge of the Message or the form in which it is presented.

Dreams
Dreams provide access to the subconscious as well as the intuitive senses. This can allow delivery and assessment of information (Messages, Signs, insight) leading to possible decisions upon reawakening. (The suggestion to explore issues, resolve problems or make decisions by "sleeping on it" really does work!)
NOTE: Keeping a dream journal can enhance your ability to search out and identify Signs, thereby allowing you to see, interpret and take action on them.

Guardian Angels
Various spiritual teachings specify the existence of an Angel uniquely dedicated to the protection of a single individual. This Angel is with the individual from birth to death and attempts to keep them from physical and spiritual harm.

Guides
Guides consist of a person's main Guide, who is constantly with them, and a team of Guides who appear depending on the situation. They

might include Ancestors, Ascended Masters, or other specialty Guides. All Guides provide invaluable guidance and wisdom.

Higher Self

One's true, whole self—the eternal being that is *wise, unconditionally loving,* and *creative.*

Intuition

The ability to know or realize something without conscious analytic reasoning. It is an innate, rather than a learned, ability. Intuition works separately from the body's physical senses and relies on six intuitive or Clair-senses to perceive and receive the Messages the person's Spirit Guides are trying to convey. As a reminder, they are:

1. **Clairvoyance or clear sense of vision**

   The ability to "see" with your mind, not with your physical eyes. It's easy for you to "see" scenes in the past, present and future. It's a bit like watching a movie while closing your eyes. You have a lot of imagination and often have vivid dreams.

2. **Clairaudience or clear sense of hearing**

   The ability to "hear" with your mind, not with your physical ears. It's natural for you to communicate with plants and animals and "hear" them respond to you. You "hear" others communicate telepathically with you, Messages that seem to be just for you, or the answer to a question you had.

3. **Clairsentience or clear sense of feeling**

   The ability to react to stimuli you receive from people or from your environment. It could be an unexpected physical sensation such as a sudden contraction in the stomach, a chill, your hair rising on your arms. It could be a negative feeling as you enter a new location. It could be sensing that the spirit of someone who crossed over is in the room with you. The emotions of others can also strongly affect you and produce a reaction in your body.

4. **Claircognizance or clear sense of knowing**

   The ability to "know" something without any prior knowledge of where the information came from or how you got it. The insight comes out of nowhere but you're certain what you "know deep inside" is accurate.

5. **Clairalience or clear sense of smelling**

   The ability to "smell" odors that have no physical source. It could be the perfume of a long-deceased grandmother or some special scent from your childhood. It usually connects us to past memories or indicates the presence of a deceased loved one. This is one of the less common ways to receive information through Clair-senses.

6. **Clairgustance or clear sense of tasting**

   The ability to "taste" something that isn't there. The taste of certain foods that remind you of a deceased loved one could indicate the presence that a loved one is trying to communicate with you. This is also a less common way to receive information.

Inner Voice (see Intuition)

Put simply, this is intuition's voice box. It can manifest in several ways—as a voice or sound that is "heard," a sense, a feeling, or an image. Whatever form it takes, the person must be open to it to receive the message.

Journaling

Also called "keeping a diary" back in the day, this is the act of writing down, on a regular and consistent basis, one's experiences, insights, feelings, and observations, solely for your own personal use (meaning not for others to read, analyze or judge). It can be extremely useful in identifying Signs that might otherwise be missed or misinterpreted.

Lucid Dreaming

As with most dreams, Lucid Dreaming (LD) occurs during rapid eye movement (REM) sleep. However, unlike all other forms of dreaming, during LD the dreamer is aware they are dreaming, sometimes to the point where they can control what occurs in the dream. Techniques have been developed that allow people to increase the likelihood of an LD, in effect making them an "on-call" capability one can use to ask for guidance from Above.

Miracle

An often–unanticipated event initiated by a Higher Being that can affect one or more persons and is often not explainable by natural or scientific laws. Sometimes called a Divine Intervention, it can involve Guides or Angels and will usually have a major positive impact on everyone it touches.

Near–Death Experience (NDE)

A near-death experience occurs when a person is either clinically dead, near death, or in a situation where death is likely or expected. People undergoing an NDE often later describe a sensation of leaving their physical bodies and "seeing" the immediate setting near their body or of travelling to other locations or dimensions (see OBE below).

Out–of–Body Experience (OBE)

A spontaneous event during which a person experiences the sensation of departing from their physical body while retaining consciousness and floating above or near it.

Precognition

The knowledge of an event that will happen in the future, obtained either via a dream or a sudden sense of "knowing."

Spirit Guides

Entities who are always watching over human beings and providing us information, guidance, Signs (including warning Signs) and Messages. They interact with different people in different ways, and different people become aware of them through different means. Some people experience a primary Spirit Guide who typically leads the communication and is supported as necessary by others where there is a specific need. Others experience regular interaction with a variety of Guides and/or Angels throughout their life as they deal with specific issues or situations.

Much has been written about Spirit Guides, their origins, capabilities, and roles. There are a wide range of approaches to this topic, depending on the specific author's spiritual, religious, or esoteric perspectives. Some authors even organize Spirit Guides into classes or categories based on rank or function. After reading this book, should you wish to gain a greater understanding of this topic, a quick trip to the bookstore or a computer data search will start you on your journey.

Spirit World

According to many spiritual teachings, human beings have a soul that is separate and apart from the physical body. Upon the death of that body, the soul journeys to the Spirit World. Spiritual teachings vary as to what happens after that. Some say that the soul comes to rest in one of two places (typically referred to as "heaven" and "hell"). Other teachings contend that the soul proceeds on its greater journey, where it continues to unfold and grow spiritually towards eventual perfection. This spiritual world is inhabited by a wide range of beings including Guides and Angels as well as other entities. Some teachings maintain that this Spirit World co-exists with the physical world, though at a higher vibrational dimension.

Synchronicity

Unexpected events occurring when two or more incidents of meaningful coincidence happen at the same time and lead to an unexpected, but positive, result. These are Messages from the Universe that the recipient is in the right place or moving in the right direction. It should be noted that sometimes the result might not be immediately apparent; it might even initially seem like a disappointment or failure.

Universe

In the Spiritual sense, the Universe is everything that is non-physical—
the Spiritual Cosmos. In terms of this book, the Universe encompasses
our Higher Self, our Guides and Angels, and the broader Spirit World.
We are one with the Universe, separated only by the limitations of our
existing in this physical dimension. Meditation and self-reflection can
help us get in closer contact with the Universe.

Acknowledgments

I first want to thank Dave, my husband, my best friend, for his constant support during the writing of this book. His patience, his encouragement, and his loving guidance helped me glide through the whole process. And the fact that he always made sure I was sufficiently fed and hydrated was no small accomplishment!

I'm so grateful for the inspiring, spiritual, and focused guidance of Christine Kloser and her fantastic "Get Your Book Done" program. Without her and the warm yet demanding support of her assistant, Jean Merrill, this book would still be a figment of my imagination. The entire GYBD team made me feel as though I was surrounded by friends cheering me on in my efforts to produce this book.

I want to thank Penny Legg for her support and advice during the development of my book and her brilliant marketing suggestions leading to the book launch.

And I send a special thank you to Carrie Jareed, the director of Capucia Publishing and Karen Everitt, Project Manager, to Lisa Canfield, my editor, and the rest of the Capucia team for their constant patience, support, and valuable advice during the publication phase. My relationship with Carrie evolved from purely professional to valued friendship, and I look forward to working again with her in the future.

My entire journey leading to this book was generated by synchronicity with the medium Paris Drake. My initial, quite dramatic encounter with him kick-started me onto my path of exploring human consciousness.

I am very grateful for the excellent, extensive guidance provided by my first mentor, Gerard Grenet. His teachings were highly instrumental in opening and expanding my awareness of the energies and entities that constantly surround us.

Also, my heartfelt thank you to Verone Garnier and Sebastien Ranucci for using their exceptional capacities to help me develop my intuition skills.

I'm grateful to Jean Angius and Marie-Ange for their invaluable friendship and for generously sharing their knowledge and wisdom.

My journey was enriched and heightened by Marcia O'Regan, who shared both her knowledge and joy of life with me.

I am so grateful for the gifted and knowledgeable professionals associated with The Monroe Institute. All the programs offered there are based on the fundamental premise of its founder, Robert Monroe, "You are more than your physical body." I wish to thank the Institute's former President, Nancy (Scooter) McMoneagle, for her friendship and constant support, as well as its excellent teachers and facilitators, Joseph McMoneagle, Beth Vaughan, Dr. Brian Dailey, Allyn Evans, Joseph Gallenberger, Lee Stone, Marinda Stopforth, Bob Holbrook, Luigi Sciambarella, and Thomas Hasenberger. They all enriched my life more than they will ever know. And finally, I want to express my gratitude to Kevin Turner, William Buhlman, Franceen King, Frank DeMarco, Charleene Nicely, and Penny Harrison. Their superb teaching and guidance helped me connect with my Spirit Guides.

About the Author

L iliane Fortna has always been, in her own words, "a late bloomer" when it comes to starting things.

Nonetheless, she has been a European model, Amazon explorer, professional dancer, and energy healer.

Born in Hanoi, Vietnam during the French–Vietnamese War to a French father and a Vietnamese mother, she was sent by her parents at 15 months old to live with her paternal grandmother on the Brittany coast of France. At age nine, she entered boarding school in Paris and has forever since considered herself Parisienne.

A professional dancer, Liliane met her husband, a USAF officer and American citizen, while working in Hawaii. After leaving Hawaii and spending four years in Washington, D.C., she quit dancing to accompany her husband on assignments throughout Asia and Europe. Wherever they lived, she did extensive volunteer work and immersed herself in the local culture and traditions.

After 15 years in Brussels, Belgium, Liliane and her husband moved to "that foreign country—the U.S.," where she finally became a proud

American citizen. She has a degree in English Literature from the University of Maryland and is fluent in three languages.

Since early childhood, Liliane has been in contact with her Guides and Angels. Following extensive training from a range of international trainers and shamans, she has been an energy healer for over 10 years. She and her husband have settled in Charlottesville, Virginia, where she continues her energy healing practice and is close enough geographically to their son and his family to enjoy her role (starting a little bit later than most) as grandmother.

How to Contact Liliane

You can find out more about Liliane at her website, www.winksfromabove.com

Email: liliane.fortna@winksfromabove.com

LinkedIn: www.linkedin.com/in/lilianefortna

Winks from Above

If you found this book to be helpful, please consider leaving a review at your favorite online retailer.

Printed in Great Britain
by Amazon

21650657R00132